Creative Writing

A Handbook for
Workshop Leaders

SUE THOMAS has taught creative writing in a wide range of settings including the Arvon Foundation, Nottinghamshire Writers' Network, Nottingham University Adult Education classes, and Rampton Hospital. She has also conducted science fiction workshops at numerous primary and secondary schools, and is currently teaching at The Nottingham Trent University where she is Course Leader of the M.A. in Writing.

Her novel *Correspondence* was short-listed for the 1990 Heinemann/East Midlands Arts Fiction Award and also achieved third place in the 1992 Arthur C. Clarke Award for Best Science Fiction novel. *Water*, her second novel was published in 1994, and she is editor of *Wild Women*, a collection of short stories about the female archetype.

This information and resource pack is the product of a research project administered by East Midlands Arts and the University of Nottingham Adult Education Department, with additional financial assistance from the Gulbenkian Foundation, the Arts Council of Great Britain and Nottinghamshire County Council Leisure Services.

Creative Writing

A Handbook for
Workshop Leaders

by
Sue Thomas

with additional contributions
from other writers who teach

Department of Adult Education
University of Nottingham

First published in 1995 by
The Department of Adult Education
Education Building
University Park
Nottingham NG7 2RD

ISBN 1 85041 078 X

Printed by The Alden Press, Oxford, England

Acknowledgements

Thanks are due to Linda Anderson, whose research contributed a great deal to the planning of this book, and also to the many writers, tutors and students whose views and wealth of experience are represented here. Thanks too to Debbie Hicks and Peter Preston who provided valuable support and encouragement. And particular thanks to the following people who kindly contributed exercises for reproduction in the book:

EDYTH BLOCK	DAVID FINE	BRENDAN MURPHY
STEVE BOWKETT	MARTIN GLYNN	KATHY PAGE
CATHERINE BYRON	JACEK LASKOWSKI	ADRIAN REYNOLDS
JANETTE DILLON	SIMON MILES	MAUREEN RICHARDSON
JANE EYRE	KENNETH MOOD	BARRY WAKEFIELD
KEVIN FEGAN	RONALD MORRIS	GREGORY WOODS

PLEASE NOTE that Section 1: Teaching Adults is adapted from *Adult Learning, Adult Teaching* by John Daines, Carolyn Daines & Brian Graham, published by the Department of Adult Education, University of Nottingham 1992. This is an excellent guide to teaching in adult education and tutors are urged to purchase a copy and study it carefully.

It can be obtained from the following address:

Publications Unit
Department of Adult Education
Education Building
University Park
Nottingham
NG7 2RD
Tel: 0115 951 4427

Contents

Preface

Recent years have seen a huge growth in the number of writers' groups throughout Britain. This expansion is partly the by-product of social and economic changes resulting in more leisure for some and increasing unemployment for others, but whatever the reason writing is proving to be a valuable vehicle of liberation and self-realisation.

For many people it has provided a route into self-expression, to finding a voice and speaking out, and a way into the making of art. As to the number of published authors who have emerged from the groups — well frankly, that's completely irrelevant. The best, most powerful and most committed authors have always written because they want to, need to, have to ... and certainly not in the pursuit of fame and fortune. They probably didn't attend creative writing groups either, although it's true to say that many may have ended up teaching them.

This book is designed to answer the needs of new creative writing tutors. It assumes that the tutors will themselves be experienced writers, and it expects that the readership will range from new authors planning to teach writing to seasoned veterans in search of new workshop ideas and techniques.

The art and craft of writing spans more than two millennia and almost every language in the world, so the reader will not be surprised that this handbook does not claim to be exhaustive. Its kernel consists of practical workshop exercises, and is supported by general information about the practice of teaching itself, the teaching of writing, a reference section, and a chapter on problems and issues. This last can be no more than a set of signposts intended to prompt tutors towards further thought and research.

Indeed, it is high time that a work was commissioned to thoroughly examine some of the ethical and philosophical problems presented by the teaching of writing. The visual and musical arts have been taught formally for centuries, first in studios and ateliers and more recently in colleges and universities, but writing has no such background and indeed still resists the assertion that it can be 'taught'. This book has been compiled from the premise that although creativity probably can't be taught it can certainly be released, encouraged, nurtured and valued.

And so the controversy rages on. As a writer and tutor myself I am subject to periods of utter scepticism about the work I do, and no more so than when my own creative ideas melt away before my eyes because I don't have sufficient time or energy to capture and explore them for myself. Sometimes, oh horror, they even end up as writing exercises rather than novels.

But then on the other hand, I enjoy teaching and have certainly learned a great deal about the skills of writing simply through having to convey them to others. It's also true that teaching and workshopping provide me with a source of income and invitations to work in various parts of the country. But lastly, and most importantly, it was joining a writing class which gave me the courage to start writing again after twenty years of silence, and maybe that's the best recommendation of all.

Sue Thomas
Nottinghamshire, February 1995

Writers
on
Teaching

_____

CATHERINE BYRON

Language is a game the rules of which we have to make up as we go along...   LUDWIG WITTGENSTEIN

Tell all the Truth but tell it slant.   EMILY DICKINSON

My initial aims with a new group are to create a sense of security — and then to drop them into a messy chaos. In creation myths the brooding god or spirit draws the world and its creatures not out of the void but out of a chaos of elements or atoms. It is vital to help individuals tap into their own teeming material, to let a bucket down into the brew of memory, obsession and association that is so efficiently lidded over in everyday life. It is also vital to control firmly but lightly what they do next, to shape the workshop session in such a way that each writer comes to some sense of what to do or where to go with their material.

That's why games are so important. The good ones have just the right mixture of rules and licence. They subvert expected patterns, but offer ways of creating new juxtapositions, new lookout posts on the familiar. With words as the medium of our particular art it is vital to surprise people into playing with language as well as with material. Words are such bread-and-butter things, such a worn coinage: so much of our early and adult training with words is concerned with the straight rails of sequential, logical prose. For poetry, or for creative prose, jumping the tracks is essential, at least to begin with. And most people need to be pushed.

So I like to spend as long as possible working orally—or even in chosen or directed silence — with a group. Writing things down comes as a secondary stage, and even that writing is usually just notes, nothing shaped or finished yet. The whole process contrives to create, in fast forward, the stages through which many poets go in the conceiving and writing of a poem: the smallish starting point, often a phrase or sense memory, perhaps a cadence nagging for attention — the uncertainty about where it is leading, or why it's come up at all — the scribbling down of what one wants to hang onto — and then the drafts that grow and change over days or months until a sense of arrival, of completion, is achieved. It is at this stage that the real critical work begins, both for the individual writer and the writing tutor: thoughts about form, about exactness of expression, about length. It often ends with the cutting of either the opening or the ending of a poem: most of us are strangely reluctant to take away that scaffolding.

Ideally, I like to lead a group through this whole process as a group, at least in the first few sessions. I like to tease and trick them into composing communal pieces, poems-by-committee with the minimum of physical writing done by them. Often I act as the group's scribe at key stages, and I take them through the stages of drafting and editing orally, or with great sheets of sugar paper, or even a black or whiteboard if available. With groups that are not yet confident with writing, or are unable to write (early primary years, people of all ages with learning difficulties) I'll stay with the oral approach the whole time, and extend it with some improvisatory drama. But I'll also extend it for as long as possible with highly-educated groups: sixth-formers deep into English Literature A Level, teachers and academics are all a big challenge to the creative writing tutor. Keep them playing and not writing for as long as possible: such groups really do need derailing!

When working with groups who cannot write at all, the quality and sincerity of the 'scribing' mentioned above is crucial. Here it is not just a warming-up stage on the way to individual writing, but the only channel for people to record and redraft their utterances. In the case of one woman in my MENCAP group, who could not even speak recognisably, it was her only channel of utterance, at least as far as poetry was concerned. It is so easy to patronise and distort someone's slowly articulated intentions by asking leading rather than opening questions, by supplying one's own words, by 'improving', by hurrying. It is vital to trust each individual as 'writer', especially at the next stage of reading back, and back again, what they have dictated, and encouraging them to change things, whether they are your misunderstandings and mishearings, or their own alterations.

Finally — and this applies to all groups — if you introduce chaos, it is very likely that, however structured the next stage is in your session, individuals will from time to time haul up shocking material in that bucket, and it will be hard to deal with it adequately or at all. Writing is risky, or should be if it is going to be any good. (And that applies to light verse as well as tragedy.) Memories of deaths and other losses sometimes break through, including forgotten incidents of abuse or violence. But writing tutors are not therapists. Remember that you are first of all concerned with writing, and hold onto that. This can help the individual concerned a great deal, and offers a route onwards for everyone. Be prepared for class members who witness others' upsets to be upset also, and even critical of what you have 'done' in raising such ghosts. Keep calm, and try to remember that it can be a major turning point for tutor and students to have to deal with difficult or sober material like this. The group will invariably assist in the support of the person who is upset: human relationships are strengthened, and with them understanding of the underlying seriousness of the art.

I have found these occasional crises difficult in my teaching, and have worried about the handling of each one. And yet, paradoxically, if such moments did not happen I would worry that my engagement with my writing students was superficial. In the teaching of writing it is vital for the working writer-tutor to remain in touch with the values of her or his own writing. It is, on the other hand, a difficult balance.

And this is yet another reason why it is essential to bring the published work of other writers into the group. It's obvious, surely, that writers as individuals need to be readers. Less widely recognised is the need for a group of writers to hear and ponder outside voices in order to counter any hothousing or just stale air. And poems such as Sharon Olds' *The Matter of This World* or Robert Frost's *Out, Out* can offer, besides much else, the pity and fear of true catharsis after a difficult session.

Catherine Byron has been a tutor on East Midlands Arts Writeaway retreats, Arvon Foundation courses at Lumb Bank and Totleigh Barton, and for the WEA, etc.; writer-in-residence to Leicestershire Adult Basic Education Service, MENCAP and several schools, including work for the W.H. Smith Poets in Schools scheme administered by the Poetry Society. She is currently external examiner for the M.A. in Creative Writing at Lancaster University.

Recent poetry collections: *The Fat-Hen Field Hospital* (1993); *Settlements & Samhain* (1993). Prose: *Out of Step: Pursuing Seamus Heaney to Purgatory* (1992).

1. Teaching Adults

I think that one's art is a growth inside one. I do not think one can explain growth. It is silent and subtle. One does not keep digging up a plant to see how it grows.

EMILY CARR

1.1 Introduction

If you were going to instruct a class on how to make an apple pie, your teaching plan would probably read something like this:

1 How to identify and collect ingredients.
2 How to make pastry.
3 How to roll and cut pastry.
4 How to peel and slice apples.
5 How to assemble pie.
6 How to bake pie.

You could provide a practical demonstration of each stage of the process, and your students would be able to measure the degree of their own success against the ultimate existence (or not) of a recognisable apple pie. Edibility would provide a further yardstick.

If, however, you're planning to teach a student how to write a short story then the situation becomes more complicated.

Firstly, of course, we're still not agreed on whether it's possible to teach someone to write a good short story.

Secondly, if we're lucky we might be able to come to some consensus on a list of components for our story — though it's unlikely we'll agree on which of them, or how many, might be used. For example:

1 Character
2 Plot
3 Dialogue
4 Description
5 Conflict
6 Resolution

All or some of these components, you explain, may be assembled in any form or permutation and still produce a short story. However, there is no guarantee that the story will prove to be interesting, entertaining, or intelligible at any level. In fact, it's possible that the only definition of a short story is that it's a piece of continuous prose from anywhere between 50 and 12,000 words in length.

And unlike the apple pie, there may be no clearly identifiable product after all your labours.

Obviously there are difficulties here in terms of planning your teaching. The student who tries to assemble the pie before peeling and slicing the apples will soon discover their mistake, but the student who writes a 5,000 word story lacking any of the components listed above (and it can be done) has a perfect right to their own creative vision. And who's to say it hasn't worked?

So how do you teach writing, and what does the process involve?

1.2 Teaching

There is no 'right way to write'. The creative writing tutor seeks to facilitate development through a combination of learning, experimentation and exploration.

In general terms, good teaching involves a clear understanding and analysis of the learning process from start to finish, plus a willingness to stop and evaluate at various stages. When teaching writing, however, there's an extra element to consider, and that is the fact that creative writing tutors are not always aiming towards a clearly specified goal. Nevertheless, the writing tutor does have practical information to impart, and must also act as mentor and guide during the students' early tentative wanderings through the creative maze.

Examine the two columns below. At first sight they seem almost to have come from two different worlds, but in certain ways they do complement and feed in to each other.

The vocabulary of teaching contains words like:

The vocabulary of writing contains words like:

The vocabulary of teaching	The vocabulary of writing
Achievement	Art
Aims	Creativity
Appraisal	Experiment
Assessment	Idea
Evaluation	Imagination
Goals	Inspiration
Method	Invention
Needs	Originality
Objectives	Response
Resources	Sensitivity

Some of the concepts in the first column can be used to stimulate and foster the ideas in the second column. For example:

Needs What do your students hope to gain from attending the group? What do they need to help them achieve it?

Aims What are their long-term expectations? These will probably include a desire to develop their imagination and improve their writing skills, maybe to win fame and fortune, but there can also be much more subtle answers to be uncovered.

Objectives These are short-term outcomes, stepping-stones pointing in the direction of more long-term aims. They can help the tutor plan a session by identifying what the students will have experienced by the end of that class. For example, an exercise based on the five senses will simply have as its objective 'to enlarge the student's perception of the physical world through the use of the five senses.'

Evaluation They may be unaware of it, but writers constantly practise assessment and evaluation. Firstly, because the processes of editing, revision and rewriting all involve rigorous and impartial reappraisal of the work in hand (see Section 2.3: Giving and receiving criticism), and secondly because effective tutors habitually monitor their teaching through regular formal and informal 'pulse-taking' (see Section 1.6: Evaluation).

1.3 Learning

How do people actually learn?

The act of learning has two parts:

1 the acquisition and storage of new information followed by
2 the retrieval and application of this new material.

The above process is ongoing throughout our daily lives,

both on a subconscious day-to-day level, and also when we consciously apply ourselves to learn something new. Such constant acquisition of new material and information results in the perpetual shuffling and re-sorting of data, and this in turn produces long-lasting changes of understanding and behaviour, and through them a ceaseless revaluation and refinement of our skills, attitudes and beliefs.

In fact, learning is so much a part of our natural lives that it would be impossible to be conscious and not learn, but it is up to us to decide whether or not to apply our learning.

How do we remember what we've learned?

Once the new data has been sorted and filed away, it will be stored in our memories and will not be available for use again until it has been retrieved (remembered).

Unfortunately, memory can sometimes be very efficient at retaining 'inconsequential' data whilst forgetting more important information. That's because memory is easily distorted by our physical and emotional perceptions, and is usually better at remembering things which interest us. And the more interesting a new thought, the more easily it will displace a memory.

How do we cope with new and unfamiliar information?

Learning happens more quickly and effectively when the new material has clear and relevant connections to what is already known. However, sometimes students need help, or just a period of time, before they can recognise and build links between recent and past knowledge.

Sometimes existing knowledge, instead of making new links, forms an obstacle to further learning, and a person may simply close themselves off and refuse to process new information.

What else interferes with learning?

Many things can interfere with learning. Physical and mental health, fatigue, stress, and emotions can all obstruct the assimilation of new data. More important, however, is the student's general disposition and character. Commitment and a desire to work hard can overcome many serious impediments to learning. Similarly, the individual who lacks self-confidence and is terrified of failure may find themselves 'blocked' and unable to improve.

What encourages learning?

There is no substitute for fulsome praise when earned, and warm, constructive encouragement if achievement is below par. Success makes for further effort, and even a little progress builds up confidence and self-esteem, leading to increased independence and creative thought.

1.4 Adult learners and their expectations

Wherever people come together we can expect to find contrast and diversity. Every individual is unique, and the older we get the greater number of unique characteristics we acquire simply by moving through life.

This makes the job of a tutor working in adult education both rewarding and complicated. It means that each student might need to follow a slightly different route at a slightly different speed, whilst demonstrating along the way a whole spectrum of strengths and weaknesses formerly acquired as products of their life experience to date.

Here are a few points to think about:

1 Adult students bring with them a considerable store of transferable skills in the form of existing knowledge and experience.

2 They also bring a set of formed ideas and opinions which may complement your teaching, or conflict with it. Perhaps they will have to be encouraged to become more flexible by doing some 'unlearning'.

3 Adults are accustomed to being responsible for themselves. They may not like being told what to do, and they are of course at liberty to leave the group whenever they like.

4 In contrast, it's ironic that older students who have been out of education for many years may expect to be told what to do, and may be confused when invited to contribute their own ideas and opinions.

5 Adult learners are often over-anxious and lacking in confidence. They are afraid of appearing foolish by failing or misunderstanding a task, and this is especially true of those with negative memories of school. For this reason they may be reluctant to contribute to class discussions, or may overcompensate by talking too much. They might

13

also be wary of undertaking risky creative experimentation.

6 Adult students are frequently keen to achieve a great deal
in a very short time, particularly those who feel they have
missed out in the past. This desire for rapid success adds
to their anxiety about achievement, and they should be
encouraged to aim for a balanced mix of long- and short-
term goals.

7 Writing may not be their first priority, but simply one of
many other commitments and interests. Many highly-
motivated students regard the writing group as a valuable oasis in the middle of a busy week, and despite their
enthusiasm may not have the time or privacy to write at
home.

8 Adults devote valuable time and sometimes money to a
writers' group. In return they will expect you to:

- know your subject.
- be able to teach it with conviction and enthusiasm.
- make efficient and well-planned use of class-time.
- make them work by providing realistic goals.
- give them regular, fair and constructive feedback.
- make the sessions enjoyable by fostering a friendly and
  supportive atmosphere.
- treat them with respect. Tutors who humiliate, criticise
  or patronise students will quickly find themselves
  without a class.

1.5 Equal opportunities and access

Adult education has always been a valuable resource for a wide range of individuals. Many people feel that they have previously missed out on educational opportunities, and very often the reasons for this are rooted in their prior exclusion from conventional provision. Having said this, adult education itself has not always been innocent of pur-veying élitism and prejudice.

By paying attention to equal opportunities, a tutor is trying to ensure that everyone, no matter what their life circum-stances, has the right to appropriate and accessible education and training. The list of those who may have suffered from restricted provision in the past includes women, members of ethnic minority communities, the elderly, the less-affluent, people with disabilities and those who are educationally disadvantaged.

Equal opportunities policy affects many areas of educational provision. If you're employed by an organisation or institu-tion they will be able to provide you with a copy of their equal opportunities policy document. Read it, and continually monitor that what it says is being put into practice.

Below are some of the ways in which you can ensure that your writers' group promotes equal opportunities.

Consider your own attitudes

Do you respond differently to students who seem different in terms of age, race, gender, ability, etc.? The expectations you have, the way you behave and the language you use may all say something about you, the way you perceive people in general and your students in particular.

Is your group organised to cater for special needs?

Those with physical disabilities need appropriate space, and those with helpers may have other specific requirements. Students with a hearing or visual impairment should be offered an optimum position near the front. You, your group, and your institution have a responsibility to accommodate students with special needs. And if you're not sure exactly what those needs are — ask!

Consider your employer's approach

Does the organisational provision cater for a wide range of people? Where are courses advertised, and in which languages? How do course times fit in with public transport, school hours and holidays? What provisions are there for the elderly and people with disabilities? Is there a crèche? Concessionary course fees?

Could your use of language be seen as offensive?

Take care that your language and attitudes do not offend. Avoid terms and images with negative overtones of race, gender, culture, sexual orientation, age or disability. Find more acceptable words and phrases.

Is your group accessible to everyone?

Could your group be arranged differently from the usual weekly meeting? Taster sessions, weekend schools, women or men only, outreach in rural areas, etc. Who is your course publicity aimed at and where is it distributed? Could it be rewritten and remarketed to show that you are keen to work with a diversity of people?

Does your teaching material reflect a sense of cultural diversity?

Are all the authors you discuss DWEMs (Dead White European Males)? Is your class already fixedly mono-cultural? Ensure that your teaching material reflects the wide range of cultural experience existing both inside and outside the classroom.

1.6 Evaluation

Evaluation is essential for tutors who wish to ensure that their teaching is effective. But there's more to evaluate than just the way the subject is taught. Students will have opinions about the tutor, about the other students, about the physical classroom environment. They may love you, but hate your teaching method! Or a student might leave the group simply because you don't allow a cigarette break — and of course on those occasions, you'll be the last person to find out why. If you ever do.

Evaluation must be carried out early in the life of the group and should become a regular feature. A form filled in on the last day of a ten-week course might benefit the tutor but will be no help at all to the students. It's more beneficial to use evaluation at the first session to identify the expectations of the students, and then again, say, at the fourth session, thus leaving enough time to make changes if the evaluation indicates they're needed. There are various ways to monitor your group, from planting an observer in the class, to private interviews, to small group discussions, to written responses.

Some suggestions for initiating verbal feedback:

- In pairs, or singly, ask students to identify 'one good thing and one bad thing' about the group.
- In small groups, ask the students to prepare a list of suggestions of ways in which the group might improve.
- Initiate a discussion about how people felt when they first joined, and how they feel now.

Written feedback — the golden rules:

- Arrange for the forms to be completed during class-time, and be prepared to leave the room if that is helpful.
- Explain the forms clearly so that the students understand what you're looking for.
- Give them enough time to write full answers.

There are many ways to compile an Evaluation Form. Here are two samples:

— SAMPLE 1 —

Please read each statement and then ring the appropriate number to show whether you: absolutely agree = 1; absolutely disagree = 10; or that your opinion lies somewhere in between (2 - 9).

The group has a very friendly atmosphere.

1   2   3   4   5   6   7   8   9   10

The work is pitched at the right speed for me.

1   2   3   4   5   6   7   8   9   10

I've gained a lot of confidence from the group.

1   2   3   4   5   6   7   8   9   10

My writing is definitely improving.

1   2   3   4   5   6   7   8   9   10

The feedback from the group is very helpful.

1   2   3   4   5   6   7   8   9   10

— SAMPLE 2 —

Please answer the questions below in the spaces provided. Please take time to express your opinions as fully as possible.

What do you like best about the group?

....

....

NB: leave plenty of space here for a full answer: 3-4 lines at least.

What do you like least about the group?

....

....

Can you suggest any new topics we could work on?

....

....

What would you like to change about the group?

....

....

Would you prefer the group to have a different day/time/ venue?

....

....

Writers
on
Teaching

KEVIN FEGAN

I work as a playwright and poet. Over the last five years, as
a full-time writer, I have written fifteen plays and three
collections of poetry. I think that is quite prolific. Yet, at the
same time, I have worked on several major residencies, run
hundreds of workshops, given hundreds of poetry readings,
edited seven anthologies, judged several competitions, co-
edited a magazine and replied, wherever possible, to endless
unsolicited mail seeking advice.

This is one of many ways to pay your gas bill as a writer. I
make no value judgements about the way a writer earns a

living; but I have fought long and hard to make my living from writing single plays — plays I want to write. This means that I work as a writer and 'enabler' (i.e. helping others with their writing). My motive has always been to develop my reputation as a writer but over the years I have come to realise that I enjoy the enabling work. It feeds my own work, forces me to continually justify my own approach to writing and reduces the chances of slipping into the nightmare world of a writer who can only write about writing.

I have always resisted the label of Teacher because I am a writer. When I first took over an evening class in creative writing all I had was a sense of my own craft and a passion for writing. No books, no exercises, nothing to help me. It was scary and I shared some of my vulnerability with the group; but I was being paid so I invented exercises as each session became a challenge to my own understanding of the craft. I am convinced that much of the craft of writing can be taught (usually self-taught).

What surprised me was that occasionally I could actually inspire people. When my passion for writing lights up my eyes I have found that I can pass it on to others like a candle flame. One woman wrote forty poems in one week following an inspired session on poetry. Her husband threatened to batter me for what I had 'done' to his wife. Apparently she was waking up in the middle of the night and scribbling into a notebook. Recognise the symptoms?

Meanwhile I was starting to sell some of my work so I decided to go full-time as a writer in 1987. Since then, most of my work as an enabler has been through a variety of residencies. Within six months I was offered a residency as a writer at Stocken Prison. It was only the third major residency at a British gaol and lasted twelve months. It was a profound experience. (If you want to know more, the Literature Department at the Arts Council of Great Britain published a "Writers in Residence in Prisons" document which outlines my experiences together with several other writers.) More to the point, I wrote three plays and a collection of poetry and edited a collection of prisoners' poetry as a result of the experience.

For eighteen months I was Resident Writer with Welfare State International. I worked with a team of artists in Barrow-in-Furness on a huge project, 'Shipyard Tales', which culminated in thirteen original shows. This residency was particularly satisfying because, in addition to the enabling brief of 'allowing the town to find its voice', I was also commissioned to find my own voice while living in the town. The result was that I wrote two of the thirteen shows. Along the way, we also ran an alternative nightclub for three months, writing and performing with local people fifteen minutes of new material each week, and performing myself in a Resident Poet slot at the club.

This type of residential work with a theatre company is product-based, unlike most creative writing workshops. The line between my own writing and my work as an enabler is often blurred by this type of work. For eighteen months I worked for Opera North on a community opera, 'Deckchair Tales', for my home town of Mansfield. I didn't write a single word of that play, but I edited and structured a group of local writers to write their own script. This is at one end of the 'community play' spectrum. At the other end is a community play I wrote recently, 'Game Challenge Level 7', for the Moss Side/Hulme/Rusholme area of Manchester. I wrote this script with a group of local writers interested in contributing to it.

Other residencies include six months as resident poet for Cheshire Arts and Libraries, playwright attached to the Theatre Studies Department at Lancaster University for a term per year over two years, and resident playwright at Market Harborough for three months.

Over the last twelve months I have been resident writer for Cheshire Arts and Libraries, this time running 'surgeries' in libraries. This is one-to-one work where local writers come to see me for a half-hour appointment with their 'complaints', or seeking advice. I have no miracle cures, I'm afraid.

I am about to start on my next residency at the Accredited Acting School in Manchester Metropolitan University. This is the first time an acting school has placed a playwright in actor training. So much of this work is breaking new ground. I have limited the residency to fifty days over the next twelve months because I am so heavily booked-up with play commissions. I love writing and I am fortunate to be able to make a living from what I enjoy.

The following is intended as an outline of my approach to running workshops and writers' groups.

Working methods (ideally a combination of all five)

1   Formal instruction in craft skills.

2   Hands-on, practical creative writing exercises.

3   Readarounds of members' work.

4   Private crits of members' work.

5   Market research by the group.

Aims

1 To help writers discover why they write.

2 To help writers learn how to edit their own work.

3 To help writers discover their strengths and weaknesses as writers.

4 To encourage writers to experiment with different writing disciplines and forms in order to find their own.

5 To confront procrastination and develop self-discipline.

6 To develop taste—i.e. to know why they like or do not like a piece of writing.

7 To learn from what others write.

Possible dangers

1 Be sensitive to the fact that not everyone attends writing workshops solely for the writing.

2 Avoid pop-psychology: it is very tempting to try and psychoanalyse people from their work.

3 Avoid back-slapping within the group but encourage praise.

4 Watch your workload: there is a tendency to take on too much, especially the private crits.

Additional comments

1 When someone expresses an opinion, encourage them to give reasons why. This creates an atmosphere in which members can say what they really feel.

2 When you know a group, take risks. Be adventurous in

your choice of material. Always treat an adult group as adults even when they might resist.

3 Be yourself and show your fallibility. You can't be expected to know everything.

4 Encourage members to share information, especially on marketing.

5 Share members' successes and rejections.

6 Listen to and try to service particular interests within the group.

Kevin Fegan's recent plays include *Excess XS* (Contact Theatre), *Game Challenge Level 7* (Moss Side community play), *Private Times* (The Library Theatre), *Lord Dynamite* (Welfare State International), *Rule 43* (Cracked Actors), *Upon St.George's Hill* (Monday Play, BBC Radio 4).

Recent poetry collection: *Matey Boy* (Iron Press).

New plays for 1994: *Strange Attractors* (Contact Theatre), *Dancing in the Ruins* (Granada TV), *The Clay Man* (site-specific in Nottinghamshire and Manchester.)

2. Teaching Writing

THE POET

When I went down past Charing Cross,
A plain and simple man was I;
I might have been no more than air,
Unseen by any mortal eye.

But, Lord in Heaven, had I the power
To show my inward spirit there,
Then what a pack of human hounds
Had hunted me, to strip me bare.

A human pack, ten thousand strong,
All in full cry to bring me down;
All greedy for my magic robe,
All crazy for my burning crown.

W.H.Davies

2.1 Introduction

Every member of your group, however shy, carries inside them their own magic robe and burning crown. That's why they're here, and that's why the first response many people will have to the title of this chapter — indeed, to the whole idea of this book — is that it's impossible to teach writing anyway. Either someone has the divine talent, or they don't, and that's that. You may subscribe to this belief yourself, and perhaps it troubles your conscience to take money for 'teaching' something that you secretly believe cannot be taught. Perhaps you feel a little superior to students who cling to your every pronouncement, or frustrated in the absence of a 'real intellectual challenge'.

For the moment, however, let's assume that your role is one of teacher/facilitator and that your interests will to some extent be naturally subsumed by the needs of the class. Whatever else you may be at other times — prize-winning poet, tree-feller, romantic novelist, unemployed executive, freelance journalist — as a writing tutor your job is simply to help other people become better writers, and to do it in the way which is most appropriate and effective for them.

Before launching into this treasure chest of techniques for releasing millions of as-yet unwritten words, let us just pause for a moment and ask 'Who is going to read them?' Writers need readers to appreciate their achievement, and readers need writers to articulate their fantasies for them. The irony of it is that generally these writers and readers turn out to be the same people.

If your students are not already avid readers, encourage them to acquire that pleasurable and addictive habit. They will soon realise that as writers they will never be alone because beside them, sucking their pens, sit the ghosts of three thousand years' worth of authors and poets. And every one of them wears a burning crown. Remind them, too, of the immortal words of William Faulkner:

> *Read, read, read. Read everything — trash, classics, good and bad, and see how they do it. Just like a carpenter who works as an apprentice and studies the mast. Read! You'll absorb it. Then write. If it is good, you'll find out. If it's not, throw it out the window.*

2.2 Who are these people and why are they here?

People join writing groups for a huge variety of reasons, and the groups themselves meet in many types of environments. These fall into four broad and inter-related categories: educational, recreational, institutional and therapeutic.

Some groups conduct formal assessment, especially if the course is part of a wider area of study, such as an English degree, and this may become increasingly widespread as the new 'A' Level in Creative Writing comes on stream. (There is no room here, unfortunately, to discuss the marking and assessment of creative writing, a topic which attracts a great deal of debate.) Most groups, however, are not tied to formal assessment procedures and can therefore evolve in very individualised directions.

The students who join writers' groups have enrolled for all sorts of reasons, many of which have nothing to do with writing. Tutors must be prepared for the fact that although they themselves may be passionate about writing, a student is only here because the car maintenance class was full, or because they hope to get rich by writing TV scripts for The Bill. That is the harsh reality of adult education today.

> "'Quantum Physics for Beginners' was cancelled, so I thought I'd try this. I like the classics best. We did *Wuthering Heights* at school — though of course that was quite a few years ago." (Cheryl, 65)

> "I've recently entered therapy and have been writing a lot of poetry. I think it might be quite good." (Anil, 19)

> "My novel's been rejected by fifteen publishers. I'd really like your opinion on where to try next." (Jo, 37)

> "My wife died last year and I need to get out and about and make new friends. No, I don't read much — most of this modern stuff is rubbish so I just don't bother with it." (Bill, 79)

> "Since I was made redundant I've been studying 'One Foot in the Grave' — it looks like money for old rope to me. I know TV comedy writers earn a fortune, so that's what I'm going to do. I've just joined to get a few pointers and some help with my spelling." (Charlie, 43)

> "All my friends say I've had such an interesting life, I ought to write a book about it. I've got the first three chapters here — shall I read them out?" (Sophya, 54)

> "I've always wanted to write, and now I've finally got up the courage. Of course, I know it'll be absolute rubbish..." (June, 29)

It's hard to believe that this motley group could have any-thing in common and yet they make up a very typical cross-section. And if you've already made up your mind as to whose work would interest you and whose wouldn't — think again because you're probably wrong. Your workshop could just be the right catalyst for Cheryl to write a future Booker Prize winner.

Because students join for different reasons they also expect different outcomes, and the tutor must be prepared to accom-modate this variety. Some simply want companionship, others want fame, or a therapeutic outlet. And everyone hopes for praise, which is where the art of constructive criticism comes in.

2.3 Giving and receiving criticism

Ask any prospective new writer what worries them most about showing their work to people and the answer will always centre upon the terrors of criticism. 'What if no-one likes it?' they cry. 'I'll never dare set pen to paper again!'

Much of this fear comes from the underlying belief that writing is a rarefied form of pure art unsullied by effort or tribulation — unlike, say, carpentry, which requires techni-cal skill in addition to artistry. Yet closer examination will soon reveal this assumption as patently untrue, and once the beginner has accepted this it will hopefully not be long before they see the benefits of both giving and receiving construc-tive feedback.

Giving criticism

- Give students regular practice in making non-emotive judgements by:

  - providing anonymous rough drafts for them to revise.
  - showing them different newspaper styles and asking them to adapt one to the other.
  - providing published stories for them to discuss analytically.
  - asking them to name one good thing and one bad thing about a poem/story.

- Encourage students to have confidence in their own opinions. No one should be allowed to get away with a plea of 'It's my fault, but I don't know what this poem is about. I suppose I'm just too stupid.' Everyone has opinions, but few can express them with assurance.

- You can build up students' confidence simply by paying attention to their comments and gently persuading them to move beyond the usual superficialities. Show that you're listening and taking them seriously by keeping good eye contact and a positive encouraging expression. Be a good listener.

- Be sensitive to the fact that they may never have discussed literature in such depth before, and you may need to help them acquire the appropriate vocabulary. Always push them beyond the first or second remarks until they are working hard to convey what they mean.

- *See also* workshop + handout on Editing and Revision in Section 3.

Receiving criticism

- Encourage open discussion of students' fears of criticism. Prompt them to think honestly about what they want to get from it. This could range from simple friendly support to rigorous editing.

- Urge students to separate their self-esteem from their writing. Failure to do this can result in pain and embarrassment, so concentrate on fostering a nurturing and constructive environment.

- Emphasise that we are not bound by sacred law to share everything we write. It may be more useful to ask for criticism only when there is a clear reason to do so. This probably won't apply to class exercises because they take place in a controlled environment where all the work produced is raw and unpolished.

- Be sensitive, though, to the fact that very emotional work sometimes suddenly emerges from an apparently innocuous exercise.

- Students should be realistic. A poem scribbled on the bus last night is going to be less polished than one which has been redrafted ten times in the last six months — therefore it may show more faults (but not, of course, necessarily — this is the problem with the Muse!).

- Writing is a two-way process, and texts are open to many different interpretations. The best way to control interpretation is to make your writing as precise as possible.

2.4 Writing as a therapeutic tool

'Writing as therapy' has two rather different meanings. It can either refer to workshops with a strong leaning towards psychotherapy, or to workshops and classes conducted in special institutions. In both respects, however, the very nature of the art means that writing tutors are often made privy to painful and emotional explorations in ways that their colleagues may never have to deal with.

Writing is commonly used as a form of healing and for self-expression at moments of intense emotion. A woman who finds herself deeply in love for the first time might find that poetry is the only vehicle through which she can express her feelings. A recently-divorced man may try to make sense of his situation by retracing his autobiography. Indeed, so many life-events, both happy and sad, find their most accurate expression through writing — bereavement, divorce, child-birth, adolescence, estrangement, marriage — the list is endless.

On occasion, the inner exploration which arises naturally when writing may unleash an unexpected degree of distress, and one which can move beyond the tutor's expertise and into the area of psychotherapy. Conversely, some students may have joined the class for that very reason, intending to use writing to deal with some past or present trauma.

In her books *Writing the Natural Way* and *Pain and Possibility*, Gabriele Rico outlines various methods for using writing as a way to tap the emotions and heal the pain which may lay buried deep inside our innermost feelings. Many of these techniques are well-known in creative writing groups: word-association, clustering, and imaging, but although such ideas form the basis of a wide range of workshop exercises, they are generally used as simple sparks to creativity and are not pursued in any depth by the tutor.

To use writing as therapy means to deliberately focus on and return to certain key images and to develop them in significant directions. It can be risky. It's like following a piece of string without knowing how long it is or where it may lead. The rewards can be high, but so can the trauma such activity may provoke. For this reason, the tutor who uses these methods must be aware of possible dangerous outcomes and furthermore should be equipped to handle them.

Writing as therapy can also refer to writing workshops in hospitals, hospices and prisons, where the very act of writing is as much of a therapy as the material itself. And not just the writing, but also the regular meetings, the coming-together of the class, the interaction with the tutor as a representative of the outside world... all of these are part of the 'therapy'. Sometimes special interest groups may be formed to help participants deal with past sexual and physical abuse, or bereavement, or terminal illness.

Script-writer Rosie Cullen spent eighteen months as Writer-in-Residence at the Pastures Psychiatric Hospital in Derbyshire. The hospital was designated for closure, and her post was designed to ease the passage of patients into the community. During her residency, a researcher made a comparative study of her work with more traditional occupational therapy and concluded that Rosie's work was more effective. It was, in fact, more therapeutic than activities which were avowedly intended as therapy because the writers were not being perceived as patients. They were taken seriously as writers, perhaps for the first time, without any burden of therapeutic expectation loaded on to the project.

The therapeutic applications of writing can be very rewarding for both students and tutors, but they also present a specialized challenge which should not be underestimated (see also Section 4.3: Writing as therapy).

2.5 Literary matters

Encourage your students to break through the élitism surrounding the study of the arts in this country by helping them to see themselves as part of the literary community.

Every writer in your group is a literary practitioner. Don't be afraid of the phrase — it doesn't make judgements, it simply describes the act. Remind your students that by starting to write they're joining a creative community which stretches way back in time, so why not become informed about the things that others have already found out? (see Section 4.6: Should writers read?)

Be aware that many of your older students will have suffered at the hands of English teachers who believed in High Art as something above and beyond the understanding of the common people. Those days are now (almost) gone.

It's true that some literary philosophers can be obscure and difficult to read, but there are plenty of other practitioners extremely capable of translating complex theory into everyday concepts. Most contemporary writers and critics see themselves as part of a wider media culture which includes film, TV and radio. They move between art forms, borrowing and translating ideas from one to another. Some have set out on an adventure to discover what comes after fiction. Is the novel dead, they ask? (After all, it was only born three hundred years ago.) Some have left paper behind altogether and now work directly with computer software. Some make poetry with no words, only sounds or shapes, others make films with no pictures. Experimentation goes on apace, but don't forget more established literature. Why not spend a session looking at the conventions of Greek drama, for example?

Writers should also understand that a story cannot come properly alive until it is read, and that every person reads it differently. There's no 'right' or 'wrong' way to interpret a story. Your gender, class, race, age — everything that makes you an individual — affects your understanding and perception of art.

Encourage your students to attend author readings and discussions, and to tune in to radio and TV programmes about literature. All the time they should be listening for items which relate to their own efforts: for example, an author on the radio complains that the kids always interrupt his poetry-writing; an editor laughs about the writer who never finishes a novel until constantly harassed; another author confesses that she can't spell, etc. And why not book a local author to visit the group for a reading and discussion? Funds to pay for such events are often available from local authorities or Regional Arts Boards.

Look at different genres and types of writing. There are dozens to consider, but have you ever chosen one to research and study? Travel-writing, biography, autobiography, food-writing, reviewing, advertising, informational writing, fairy-tales, news-reporting, feature articles, concrete poetry, literary criticism, romance, science fiction, crime, adventure, jokes, performance poetry, children's writing of all types, educational writing, thrillers, diaries, oral story-telling, memoirs, humour.... Students can choose a topic to research and then present their findings to the group.

Finally, emphasise the fact that by experimenting with some literary ideas your students are not copying the products of so-called 'successful' authors. They're simply wandering through the factory and playing with a few machines.

2.6 Effective presentation

Anyone who has been to school or college, or attended a public lecture or reading, or visited the theatre or anywhere else which is engaged in communicating to a live audience... in fact, anyone who has ever listened to someone else trying to tell them something... will already be something of an expert in the skills of self-presentation. In other words, you already know how it feels to be on the receiving end of a speaker who mutters, or gabbles, or whispers, or is so nervous that they cannot meet the gaze of their audience.

The theory of communication involves a huge range of aspects, but they all come down to the same idea: messages must not simply be sent, they must also successfully arrive. Anything which interferes with the correct transference of the message is termed as 'noise'. This does not simply refer to sound but indeed anything which prevents accurate reception. For example, if someone speaks to you in Japanese the message may not get through because you don't understand Japanese, or because you cannot hear their voice, or because you're tired and concentrating only on the prospect of a coffee-break, or because you're distracted by the spinach stuck between their teeth.

If you're inexperienced in this area you'll probably find it useful to read around the subject of public speaking, but meanwhile here are a few basic points to consider:

- Can all of your students see you from where they're sitting?

- Can they all hear you?

- Are you speaking too fast?

- Are you constantly avoiding making eye contact?

- Are you paying more attention to some students than to others?

- Are you cramming in too much information at a time?

- Does your session have a clear structure in terms of planning and timing?

- Are you repeating yourself?

- Are you talking too much or for too long?

- Do you give students the chance to ask questions?

- Do you answer those questions satisfactorily?

- Are you conveying a sense of enthusiasm?

- Could your voice sound a little monotonous? Do you 'um' and 'er'? (Tape yourself, and find out.)

- If you write on the board or a flipchart, is the writing large enough to be legible by the whole class?

Note:

All of the points above could equally refer to the occasions when students read aloud in class, and you might like to plan a session designed to convey some of this information for their own use.

Writers
on
Teaching

MARTIN GLYNN

Bringing it out

On being asked to write an article about so-called creative writing, I am faced with certain problems. Namely, can any of us teach anyone to write in a creative way? Over the years I have re-defined my perspective, enabling me to be focused around exactly what I can or cannot contribute to the development of ideas coming from a range of people with numerous skills which have yet to surface. Therefore I would like to say that I see myself as someone who facilitates, directs and extracts the creative energies from the individuals I work with, providing them with skills which can provoke them into expressing the creativity they already possess, but with a bigger range of options to choose from.

I have worked with most types of groups, from the mentally and physically handicapped, through inmates in a maximum security prison, to lecturers, undergraduates, and other writers. I have found that there are certain basic rules which are quite successful:

Creation of the right environment

1   Chairs laid out informally.
2   Background music when applicable.
3   Listening to the views of others.
4   Placing value on each contribution.
5   Doing what I ask everyone else to do.
6   Asserting the tone of the workshop at the beginning and sticking to it.

One of your most important assets is your own personality — vital in terms of motivation and self-determination. Recently I undertook a residency working with African/Caribbean inmates at Long Lartin maximum security prison, and struck up a great rapport... the reason... I had the same cultural background, I related to their experiences, plus I appealed to a sense of who they were, which made them motivated enough to want me to work with them. Therefore you must look at yourself and know how to market what you have to the audience you want to be on the receiving end of your own knowledge and skills. I have witnessed too many examples of misplaced tutors who cannot cope, or do not motivate anyone, yet they are good writers. A good facilitator can and does work with any group, but an assessment of your strengths and weaknesses is paramount in identifying exactly what you are capable of giving to others.

A very important area to deal with positively is the first time you fail to get through to someone. Although they may be difficult you still can't avoid feeling rejected. It can be disruptive, but more importantly, it can also hurt! I have found that I cannot always get through to someone unless I find out the root of their unease. So I will spend time finding out what the individual isn't getting from my methods, and allow them the freedom to discover the advantages of keeping your own identity within a group setting. If you have a good rapport with the group, allow that group to share the rejection by placing responsibility on everyone for group dynamics, as you are a facilitator not a dictator. You are part of a group and should show a willingness to also learn from those who are there to learn from you.

Bringing out the best in people is important, so motivation is a key component to building trust. To do this, you must like people, young people, old people, black people, etc. Having the ability to use humour effectively can help. It is also vital that you are knowledgeable about what you are trying to do, so that students take pride in knowing that they are with someone who knows. A constant look at your methods is crucial. You may not see yourself as boring or awkward or aggressive, but others might. I am very careful about my self-image, and I always ask students what they think a novelist or a poet looks like, as there are preconceived notions about style and behaviour which may need to be challenged. Regarding positive reinforcement, I always allow for adequate question/answer sessions, as well as a small time for evaluation, because most of all students must enjoy what they are doing, and despite the hardships of the processes, feel rewarded for their efforts with positive feedback from you and the group, building confidence along the way.

Finally, it is my firm belief that we have many stories inside our heads which need to be brought out, shared, and enjoyed by as many people as possible. Not everyone can read or write or perform, but may be excellent story-tellers. This means that not only should we be helping everyone to express themselves, but recognise that we too must continuously re-educate ourselves, and be open to new ideas, techniques and methods, meaning that we should all engage in reading, seeing, hearing and enjoying the works of others. By doing this we will have many more things to offer those who need our help.

Martin Glynn has conducted over 1500 workshops in many parts of the world, within a multitude of different settings. He is widely published in his own right, as well as in magazines and anthologies. He is currently engaged in developing screenplay ideas.

3. Workshop Exercises

You can't wait for inspiration. You have to go after it with a club.

JACK LONDON

3.1 Introduction

The exercises in this section have been collected from a wide range of experienced tutors working in a variety of situations from higher education to community groups to hospitals and prisons. There are very simple ideas for students just beginning to write, plus more complex exercises aimed at developing a confident voice, and further suggestions on teaching particular styles and forms. Also included are suggestions for discussion topics, a sample exercise, a list of props and a series of workshop exercises with accompanying handouts.

A workshop exercise is only as effective as its leader. Students attend writers' groups to learn, but they also come to be inspired, and daunting though this may seem their success may depend largely on your own charismatic personality! It would be misleading and unrealistic to suggest otherwise, and that is why Section 1 focused upon general teaching and group skills. The exercises collected here have worked for other tutors but may need adaptation or 'customisation' before they work for you. Use them as the basis for experimentation and further invention.

As a tutor you don't have to be all things to all people, and over a period of time you'll develop your own preferred style and interests. Your personal writing passions will begin to show, and so long as you don't allow them to dominate the class they'll provide a flavour of commitment which may be absent in more impersonal styles of teaching.

Don't worry too much about other specialisms. If the group is desperately keen to find out about screen-writing, for example, it may be possible to arrange a session with a tutor more knowledgeable than yourself.

For many students, the writers' group meeting will be the only occasion in the week when they set pen to paper and they'll feel unfulfilled if they go away without having written anything. Others would prefer to write at home and spend the group time in reading out and getting feedback. Yet others want you to spark them off with an exercise to which they will add another ten pages at home. It's easy to expect too much of a group, and equally easy to expect too little. Adults who are bored or understretched may either quietly leave or, more worryingly perhaps, simply adjust their standards downwards to suit.

Many of the exercises in this book may seem at first to be very basic, but the trick lies in knowing how to expand and develop them to suit your class. As we've seen, groups of adult learners often contain students of widely disparate expertise and commitment and this is why each exercise needs careful thought beforehand.

> *In my own experience, nothing is harder for the developing writer than overcoming his anxiety that he is fooling himself and cheating or embarrassing his family and friends. To most people, even those who don't read much, there is something special and vaguely magical about writing, and it is not easy for them to believe that someone they know — someone quite ordinary in many respects — can really do it.*
>
> JOHN GARDNER.

3.2 Writing-related activities

Talks and discussions

- Not all of the group's time needs to be spent writing and reading out. It's a good idea to produce some written work every time, but just occasionally the major part of the session could be spent either in an informative presentation or in discussion of writing-related issues.

- Students can also be encouraged to contribute by bringing along newspaper cuttings and by collecting bons mots on writing for the edification of the class. Talks and presentations can, of course, be given by either yourself or a student or group of students. If you have access to a video you could show a documentary about writing.

- You could ask students to:

  - prepare a five-minute talk on their favourite author
  - find a quotation about writing to share with the class
  - talk about the things which fire and inspire their writing
  - bring a favourite poem to read out and talk about
  - compare news reports in different papers, for example *The Sun* and *The Times*
  - talk about their favourite childhood book.

- You could give a talk on:

  - specific authors/poets/playwrights, etc.
  - current writing trends and debates
  - the history of fiction/poetry/printing, etc.
  - the differences between genres
  - the editorial and publication process
  - self-publishing
  - or you could prepare a discussion around one of the Problems and Issues raised in Section 4.

Props

- Almost anything can be used as a prop to start people writing, and many tutors keep a boxful of found objects for this purpose. But a single perishable item — a small brown loaf, for instance! — can be equally stimulating to the imagination. Here are just a few suggestions:

exotic fruit
art postcards
coloured and textured papers
music
jewellery
old letters
an empty cardboard box
a sealed box
a cookery recipe
a bag of penny sweets
perfumes and smells in variety
flowers — fresh, plastic, silk
machinery (working and broken)
clocks
calculators
telephones
something very old —
    a book
    piece of clothing
    ornament
something very new —
    hi-tech inventions
    plastics
    metals
    an item of abstract art
a doll
vegetables in their earthy state
newspaper articles and photographs
tactile items —
    fur
    silk
    velvet
    leather
    satin

crimplene
stones
wood
leaves
stuffed animals
children's toys
museum specimens
family photographs

... or why not take your group on a walk around the local area? Even just the weather, or the building where you meet could provide inspiration.

3.3 Planning a session

Planning is vital. New tutors should always prepare a plan even if they don't intend to stick to it.

Planning is vital — but then so is flexibility. You should aim for an atmosphere which is directed and purposeful and yet remains sensitive to swings of topic and mood.

Think also of your own experience as a student or group participant. What's important for you in those situations? Often it may have nothing to do with the content or the quality of the teaching, but may be more about physical comfort.

Make sure:

- that you allow time for a break half-way through the session
- that there are facilities for making tea, coffee, etc.
- that there is easy access
- that smokers have somewhere to go during the break (these days the consensus will probably be to ban smoking during the session)
- that there are toilet facilities
- that the room is not too cold, hot, noisy, stuffy, etc.
- that the furniture is suitable and of the correct height.

Remember

There is no such thing as a 'typical' writers' group. First, because the nature of the beast depends upon its parts, and second because there is no formal syllabus or received wisdom to follow. Some groups never write during the session, others write all the time. Some study technique, others don't. Some foster rigorous and intelligent criticism, others prefer gentle encouragement.

Do's and don'ts

Do   organise the room to your satisfaction. A circle, with or without desks, is best. (Remember that the caretaker might expect you to replace furniture at the end of each session.)

Do   make sure that electrical equipment (cassette players, videos, etc.) is set up and working before the session starts.

51

Do	tell the group before they begin an exercise if you'll be asking them to read out. Some exercises are clearly going to produce very private responses, so relieve any anxiety about self-exposure before they start writing.
Do	establish an atmosphere of quiet concentration during writing time.
Do	make sure you arrive ten minutes early in order to arrange the room and any possible materials.
Don't	agree to take home and read every word your students write. It's unpaid and time-consuming work. Decide on a policy for this and stick to it.
Don't	gabble! especially when explaining an exercise. Make sure everyone clearly understands the task being set.
Don't	suddenly stop everyone writing unless to do so is part of the exercise. Give a couple of minutes' warning, then time to finish the sentence.
Don't	allow the group to feel dominated or threatened by difficult students (see Section 4).

3.4 Three sample session plans

Here are three very different session plans, devised to fit an evening meeting running from 7.30-9.30. Don't, however, expect two hours to be the usual length. A lot of sessions run for one and a half hours, or an hour and forty-five minutes, and of course can take place during mornings and afternoons as well as evenings. You may also be asked to run a whole day session.

Each sample session opens with the same format: introducing new members; a run-down of the plan for the evening (not applicable in C, where the group does the same thing most weeks); an exchange of information where tutor and students share details of competitions, new books and magazines about writing, TV and radio programmes, etc.

— SESSION A —

A range of activities including opportunities to write, discuss, and learn. This type of programme is flexible and can be continued the following week, or for homework, if you run out of time, but it does require some advance planning. A varied session like this is useful with a new or mixed ability group. It allows people to interact and to progress at their own speed.

7.30   Introduction: new members; what we'll be doing tonight; general information, competitions, etc.

7.40   Ten-minute writing exercise based on inventing a character.

7.50   Readouts (either to the group or in pairs). Discussion.

8.05   Tutor draws together the points raised and elaborates upon them.

8.15   Coffee break.

8.35   Class is told that the character they have just created now fully exists. They must now fill in the handout Building a Character (*see page 111*).

8.45   Readouts and discussion.

9.00   Intensive writing time for further developing this evening's piece.

9.25   The tutor quietly ends the session.

— Session B —

This class focuses more closely around the tutor as teacher and purveyor of knowledge. Its relatively formal environment is useful for introducing complex or unusual ideas, and can also provide a safe atmosphere for experiment.

7.30   Introduction: new members; what we'll be doing tonight; general information, competitions, etc.

7.40   Mini-lecture about the technical and artistic aspects of character development supported by examples of other authors' writing (either read aloud, or on handouts).

8.05   Time for questions.

8.15	Coffee break.
8.35	Students begin their own piece of writing, based on what they've just learned.
9.00	Readouts and discussion.
9.20	Tutor summarises the evening's work and closes the session.

— SESSION C —

This group has the advantage of 'forcing' students to write outside the class, and then examining the resulting material in some detail. It requires good listening skills and a high degree of concentration.

7.30	Introduction: new members; general information, competitions, etc.
7.40	Students have each completed a writing task during the week, and now they take turns to read it out to the group. Each piece is discussed before moving on to the next, and the tutor expands upon issues raised as they go along.
8.15	Coffee break.
8.35	Continuation of above.
9.20	Tutor draws together the evening's work, and sets the writing task for next week.

3.5 Sample Exercise

This exercise is used by Maureen Richardson and here she explains it in minute detail. Although it's based on a very simple idea it can be used to prompt students' inventiveness and imagination to a high degree of sophisticated thinking. (I have added some explanatory remarks.)

— *HANDS AND FEET* —

Purpose

This is a continuous exercise which can be used in separate parts but achieves more when used in the following way because it builds upon each stage.

It's always useful to be aware of possible development routes for the exercise you've chosen.

It's a fun way of helping new writers find their way in and will help the inexperienced break down the 'But I can't write' or 'I'm not as good as the rest of the group' syndrome. At the same time it assists more able writers either to practise or to write under pressure, in company and with a time limit. Often it can jolt writers out of ruts such as 'I'm good at descriptive stuff so that's what I do' or 'I've never tried dialogue because I just know I can't do it', etc. It also demonstrates how to build and portray a character.

Most groups contain a diversity of skills and experience. Make sure that your exercise will be useful for all.

What will they learn?

Stage One

Method

Tell the class to place a sheet of paper on the floor, take off one shoe, and draw a quick rough outline around that foot. They can now replace their shoe and settle down to answering some of the following questions:

A little light entertainment, used very sparingly, can be a friendly icebreaker.

1   Think of someone you know or knew well and write that person's name at the top of the sheet of paper with the drawing of the foot on it.

Beginners often find it easier to work from real people. Of course, they can make up a character if they prefer.

2   Put in one corner a list of all the different footwear you think that person might own.

3   What size shoe do they take?

Do they look after their shoes?

Where did they buy them?

Do they cobble their own shoes, or have them mended, or just wear them out?

Are the shoes uncomfortable?

Can you see the shape of bunions when the shoe is empty?

Do they smell? Of what? leather, polish, dubbing, talc, BO?

These questions are designed to make the student think hard about the topic, and to move them away from cliché.

4 How did that person walk in these shoes when they were young and older?

What about the physical attributes of their bare feet: overgrown cuticles, dirty nails, corns, hard skin, veins etc?

Writing doesn't always have to be pretty. We're looking for truth, honesty and accuracy here.

5 Does that person have any foot-related habits like foot-tapping with impatience, cleaning toecaps on trousers, etc?

6 What do they use their feet for?

Digging, football, dancing, marching, driving?

Are they light or heavy on their feet?

7 Now draw around your hand and again put the name of a real person on the sheet.

Repetition of the major elements of the foot exercise allows students to improve on their first attempt.

8 Fill in the finger and thumb spaces with activities that person would use their hand for, e.g. playing the piano, smacking children, washing dishes, etc.

9 Now imagine that the hand has gone missing and fill in the palm space with details of what it looks like and what makes it individual: rings, watches,

Students may find that they are starting to jump the fence of reality and may even be making things up by now. That's fine. The real person was only a springboard for their imaginations.

bracelets, tattoos, arthritic joints, shape of nails, texture of skin, age spots, scars, nicotine stains, etc.

10 Which mannerisms does this person have? Do they rotate their thumbs, rub their cheek when worried, keep their hands very still, etc?

11 Using their notes, each student describes their character to the group, and discussion arises naturally alongside. Topics might include:

Discussion is invaluable in guiding the students' understanding about what they have achieved.

- It's useful to know more about your character than you actually intend to use.

- What happens when reality turns into fiction?

- You can introduce a discussion about logical factual amassing being a left side of the brain activity and creative utilising being a complementary right-hand-side brain function. This can be encouraging to new would-be writers who have only ever written reports for years and despair of ever becoming creative.

You can also impart new information...

- Make sure you remark encouragingly on the number of features each student has found.

...boost confidence...

- Point out how this exercise has 'drawn' real people, yet basic visual clues like hair colour, etc. are often still unknown.

... and convey technique.

Stage Two

1   Now it's time to develop the characters more fully, for which students can use either their own or borrow other people's.

2   First, everyone writes an idea for a setting on scraps of paper which are then pooled and drawn out. Examples might include a bustling fish quay, a party, a factory, a country bus, a lift. To complicate matters further you can also draw lots for the weather, the year, objects to include, etc.

This constant pooling of ideas may seem anathema to many writers, but it is very useful in kick-starting the imagination, and it's always pleasurable to hear what someone else has done with your idea.

3   Finally, lots are drawn for situations, e.g. one of the characters has suddenly gone dizzy, or shares something with the other, or threatens to harm the other, etc.

4   Students then write up the scene in whatever style they wish. In group time this will probably mean enforcing a time limit — or the task can be used as homework.

Now comes the time when discussion ends and the group concentrates on quiet writing.

5 Everyone reads out what they have written, unless it is very personal. As they have written under pressure with no real editing time we alter our usual rule of giving constructive criticism either by limiting it or dispensing with it altogether or perhaps inviting self-criticism, e.g. 'I must alter that word, I've used it four times' or 'Gosh, I was out of breath reading that out, I must break it into shorter sentences.'

It's always useful to set the rules re criticism, and this invitation for self-criticism is especially effective. Take care, though, that it's constructive and not just self-deprecating.

Stage Three

1 Students can now use all this as preparation towards a chapter of a novel, an article, poem, or short story. Sometimes we vary this by making it a radio, stage or TV play.

By now students will be developing this work at home, and it may soon become too long to read to the group in its entirety. However they can always discuss their progress, read out selected extracts, or pass copies around the group.

3.6 Workshop exercises

Each exercise has been roughly coded (see below) with an indication of the length of time you might expect it to take, but since most involve reading out or discussion you should adjust your plans according to the number in your group.

Needless to say, a group of six will take much less time to read out than a group of twenty. In fact larger groups may benefit more from paired readings and discussions than from time-consuming readarounds.

The exercises are presented in random order to allow you to compile your own menus and lesson plans. Some have obvious connections and similarities, but there is also a wide variation in scope which can be adjusted further where desired.

If your group is very inexperienced, or has special needs, you might find it best to use only short and fairly basic exercises until their confidence has increased. Such groups also generally enjoy a lot of variation and plenty of props to stimulate their imagination.

You might like to plan an entire term's programme using exercises of increasing complexity, or just dip in and out of the selection at your leisure.

Code	Average Completion Time
-15	15 minutes or less
-45	between 15-45 minutes
45+	more than 45 minutes

Materials

Students should bring an A4 pad and a pen to every class, and should be encouraged to carry a small notebook with them at all times.

Extra preparation or materials are indicated where appropriate.

— WORKSHOP 1 —

Purpose   To warm students up on the first session, and to convince them that they have imaginations; to show that you don't have to have a story whole in your head before you write it down, and also to induce a sense of wonder.

Method   I normally do this one after a short discussion about students' insecurities with reference to writing. Someone always says that they can't think of what to write.

Ask the students to quickly think of a single sentence, just one, and write it down. Wait for everyone to finish. If anyone is stuck (very rare) give them one, written down for them to copy out. When this is done, tell them to read their sentence and then write the next sentence. And then the next. Three is enough. Read around quickly, with no criticism. I make the point that if a fourth or a fifth or a twentieth sentence had been asked for, they would have been able to write it.

-15   KATHY PAGE

— WORKSHOP 2 —

Purpose   Fun with words.

Method   Draw with words — swan, bird, dog, house — then fill in the shapes with words to do with the subject.

-15   KENNETH MOOD

— WORKSHOP 3 —

Purpose   To encourage people who feel wedded to one form of writing to try out another.

Materials   A pre-selected poem or a selection of newspaper cuttings.

Method   *either* find a poem with an elusive narrative content (like some of Eliot's shorter poems, for example) and ask the class to write a story around it.

or approach the task the other way round, by giving the class newspaper cuttings or other pieces of narrative prose, and asking them to write a poem from that material.

-45   JANETTE DILLON

— WORKSHOP 4 —

Purpose   Using the five senses in descriptive writing.

Materials   One or more pictures.

Method   A given painting or photograph. The student imagines being present within the picture and describes each sense.

-15   EDYTH BLOCK

— WORKSHOP 5 —

Purpose   To teach close sensual observation.

Materials   One satsuma or orange per person, or other suitable food!

Method   Place a fruit in front of each person, but do not allow them to touch it. Instruct the class to write extensive notes about what they can see, and possibly smell, of the fruit before them.

Now instruct them to pick up and examine their fruit, but they should not yet peel it. As before, tell them to make extensive notes about texture, shape, scent, appearance, etc. Next, they may peel and segment the fruit, making more notes about their discoveries.

Finally, they may be permitted to eat the fruit and make more notes about taste, temperature, etc.

-15   SUE THOMAS

— WORKSHOP 6 —

Purpose   Starting-point.

Method   Ask everyone to think up a first line, and others to write down each first line as members of the class read them aloud. Then ask people to

either

carry on writing from someone else's first line

or

construct the outline of a piece that could follow on from someone else's first line.

-15   JANETTE DILLON

— WORKSHOP 7 —

Purpose   An introductory exercise to get to know each other's names.

Method   Write your name vertically on a piece of paper, then use each letter as the first letter of a word until you have a sentence which describes you. For example:

> S-o
> I
> M-ight
> O-rdinarily
> N-ot
> M-eet
> I-ndividual
> L-ives
> E-xpressing
> S-ense

-15   SIMON MILES

— Workshop 8 —

Purpose   Writing skills: precise observation.

Method   Direct students' attention to various features and objects within the room. Ask them to write down two material qualities and one adjective in response to each object. For example:

Blackboard rubber — wood, felt — dusty
Wall — cement, paint — cracking
Window — glass, grime — greasy
Discuss results in large or small groups.

Apply the same formula to other subjects, e.g. faces, clothes, attitudes and abstractions.

-15   JANE EYRE

— Workshop 9 —

Purpose   Freeing the imagination/providing starting points.

Method   One or two letters of the alphabet are offered as a stimulus to write a short piece within a time limit (e.g. five minutes).

Encourage random response — for example, produce three varied short pieces about the letter 'A'. Pieces can be anything — prose, poetry, lists — using any kind of technique, e.g. statement, story, alliteration, etc.

Participants read aloud one they feel happiest with. Results discussed.

The exercise can be left at this point, or efforts revised and refined after discussion.

-15   JANE EYRE

— WORKSHOP 10 —

Purpose   Writing skills: image building.

Method   Invite participants to write down a list of clichés and to complete them. E.g:

> As wise as....
>
> As cold as....
>
> As innocent as....
>
> As black as....
>
> As white as....
>
> As hard as....

Make three alternative endings to each simile. Discuss the qualities of each new image. This exercise can be done individually or in pairs or small groups. Designed to develop original precision.

-15   JANE EYRE

— WORKSHOP 11 —

Purpose   Writing skills. Groundwork for building images (word association).

Method   A colour is suggested as a stimulus, e.g. white/black/ blue, etc. Participants write down their colour on line one of a sheet of paper. Then write three concrete nouns below the word, then three abstract words associated with the colour below those to make a vertical list. Think of two adjectives for each word in the list, and write them next to the word you associate them with.

E.g. RED
      blood — life-giving, glutinous
      paint — chemical, bright
      rose — aromatic, sharp
      anger — furious, tense
      danger — pain, urgent
      fear — sweaty, trembling

Discuss the lists in pairs or small groups and cross out all the familiar clichés. Exchange lists and add new words to someone else's list, in response to their existing words. This exercise can be done individually or in pairs or small groups. It can be extended and refined by specific direction from the facilitator, and can finally result in a poem or poetic piece of writing.

-15   JANE EYRE

— WORKSHOP 12 —

Purpose   To offer practice at writing poetry which rhymes.

Method   Take the rhyming words from any poem. (Choose one without archaic end-words. The more elaborate the rhyme-scheme, of course, the more complex will your students' results become.)

Give the students this rhyme scheme to work to, using the same end-words in the same order, but filling out the lines with text of their own devising. Do not specify any particular metric requirement or line length; let students vary these as they choose.

Clearly, the given end-words will help to determine the poem's topic, but will not dictate it.

-15

GREGORY WOODS

— WORKSHOP 13 —

Purpose   Finding a voice — enabling the writer to write from different perspectives.

Method   You might want to relax before you do this, and closing your eyes can help. Run through the events of today or last night in your head. See them as if a camera crew was following you about. What would they have seen? What conclusions could they have drawn from your actions and appearance? Once you've tried it yourself, try it with characters in a story you're writing. Quite often you'll find that characters have their own way of doing things and seeing them can crystallise your concept of both character and story. It can also help in deciding which words really help to get that character across, and which can be omitted.

-15

ADRIAN REYNOLDS

— WORKSHOP 14 —

Purpose   To sharpen powers of description.

Method   Choose an individual in the group — preferably someone you don't know, and describe that person in the
manner of a novelist introducing a character into a
novel, inventing a personality from appearances. Be
generous, and be careful as you will read this to the
group. As a follow-up, for a later session, study someone
away from the group — a face in a crowd/pub/place of
work — a complete stranger.

-15   RONALD MORRIS

— WORKSHOP 15 —

Purpose   To improve listening skills and ability to cooperate with
others.

Method   In pairs: one becomes amanuensis to the other who tells
a story. The amanuensis can 'take over the reins' when
the 'teller' flags; can introduce ideas, but pass back the
reins to the 'teller' on demand. Then change roles.

-45   RONALD MORRIS

— WORKSHOP 16 —

Purpose   Using the five senses in writing about people.

Materials   Enough thesauruses to go round and a selection of
pictures of people.

Method   The students use a thesaurus to identify the variety of descriptive words to be found for features, expression and general stature. Then mounted pictures of people taken from magazines are distributed, one for each student to describe.

-15   EDYTH BLOCK

— WORKSHOP 17 —

Purpose   For beginners, to help them find out what they want to write.

Method   Ask them to think of where or who they'd want to be if they weren't in the class. This is fun — after all, everyone can daydream! Each tells the group.

Then in class or — preferably — at home they write how they got there. Every which way — wannabe is fancyfree.

Share results with the group. What have they each written? Thriller, kitchen sink, romance? This should point to genre and / or style. Lots of dialogue might mean a dramatist, pale purple passages a poet.

Also ask them what they felt like while writing it. Behind any awkwardness may be a sense of power. This helps emphasise that writers within their medium are the most powerful people in the world — they tell everyone what to do, and no-one tells them. This sense of power and responsibility should lead to assurance.

-45   DAVID FINE

72

— WORKSHOP 18 —

Purpose   Basic character construction (characters make the plot; the writer makes the characters).

Method   Ask each member of the group to think of someone they've met who has intrigued them, from as recently as today to long, long ago.

Ask them to fold a piece of paper down the middle, and on the left-hand side to jot down their looks, age, job, speech.

Each group member talks about their character, trying not to mention their real name. Each group member picks someone else's piece of paper — the one which most interests them.

They each then have to write a paragraph of a story around this character. Suggest on the right-hand side of the paper they jot down what each characteristic means in terms of behaviour.

In their story paragraphs they're almost bound to have another character. This leads on to the next stage by illustrating that characters do not exist in isolation and are usually defined by other characters.

-45   DAVID FINE

— WORKSHOP 19 —

Purpose   To explain the idea of Point of View. Think of 'E.T.' filmed with the camera at three feet high to obtain the point of view of a small child. How can we work this into writing?

Method   Ask the group to each think of something interesting which has happened to them within the last month — the first thing that comes into their mind. They can make brief notes if they like.

Then ask them to tell the group. (This will help secure the narrative flow without fixing it by writing it down.) Everybody invariably will narrate it in the first person — 'I saw this...'.

In class or at home, ask them to write their incident from another's point of view. It need not necessarily be a participant — it could be a child or a workmate, or just an anonymous third person (the only way, if the incident involves just themselves).

When sharing them in the group, focus on how it felt to move from one person to another. This is the real point of point of view.

-45   DAVID FINE

— WORKSHOP 20 —

Purpose   'Families are like road accidents; everyone witnesses something different.' Why? Because that's how characters interrelate.

Method   Each student develops a character by matching characteristics to attitudes (e.g. cleanliness is next to godliness) and keeps adding information until they know their characters well enough to know how they would vote, do the washing up, drive to work, react to a relationship breakup, etc. At this stage they should be able to predict their character's behaviour, past present and future, and they will have built a biography.

Then create other characters who move in the same environment — how do they all relate to each other?

Note: this exercise demonstrates that the relationships between characters will naturally embody the conflicts which make stories interesting. This is a better approach than simply inventing a conflict and then building a story to fit.

-45   DAVID FINE

— WORKSHOP 21 —

Purpose   Demonstrating verse forms.

Method   Riddles, 'Imagine yourself to be a particular object and describe yourself in riddle form'.

Other very specific types of writing (clerihews, limericks, villanelles, etc.) can be set for individual sessions, with a topic prescribed, if desired.

-45   JANETTE DILLON

— Workshop 22 —

Purpose   Feeding the imagination.

Materials   Newspaper cuttings.

Method   Take in newspaper cuttings and ask people to write pieces arising out of the story in any other form. This can be specific: e.g. 'Write the diary entry written by the girl abducted in the story', etc; or general: 'Re-write the newspaper story in poetry, prose, or drama from any imagined perspective.'

-45   JANETTE DILLON

— Workshop 23 —

Purpose   To give practice in factual writing.

Method   The group holds a 'Question Time' discussion. Questions are provided by the students, then discussed by anyone who wants to make a contribution.

Students make notes as the discussion progresses, then all write up an account of the proceedings and compare the finished products for accuracy.

-45   EDYTH BLOCK

— Workshop 24 —

Purpose   Useful Gestalt workshop technique for kick-start writing based on 'inner' thoughts.

Method   Sit group members in pairs facing each other. Ask them to talk in turn quietly to partner, noticing first one thing 'out there' in the environment, then one thing 'in here' within themselves. The partner listens without comment. Then swap roles. Continue back and forth until group leader says stop.

Then, without discussion, write down as much as possible from the experience of both partners — and how did it feel! Now use those notes as a basis for writing.

-45   BARRY WAKEFIELD

— WORKSHOP 25 —

Purpose   Feeding the imagination.

Materials   Personal objects brought by students.

Method   Ask group members to bring along to the session an object which belongs to them and which has great significance to them — and to keep the object hidden until asked to reveal it.

Sit the group in a circle and ask them all to reveal their objects and place them on view for all to see (no talking!).

Spend a few minutes in silence looking at the objects, taking in shape, colour, texture, etc. — still in silence — no touching.

Ask them to each choose one object (not their own) to focus on and then write on the theme: 'What would that object mean to me if I were its owner?'

-45   BARRY WAKEFIELD

— WORKSHOP 26 —

Purpose   For finishing a workshop or course, especially one where group cohesion has been strong.

Method   Sit group in a relaxed atmosphere and guide them through individual thoughts on all the times they have had to say good bye/let go/lose someone or something. Then get them writing.

Warning   This can create strong emotions, and may be best as a penultimate activity followed by a lighter exercise. Obviously the technique can tap into grief and must be handled sensitively.

-45

BARRY WAKEFIELD

— WORKSHOP 27 —

Purpose   To improve the narrative drive of a story. This exercise also helps people to give and receive criticism since not only are they not working with a finished product, they are helping to finish it.

Materials   Postcard-sized blank cards.

Method   Each student notes down on a piece of card the key event of the story. Then on another card, the circumstances which brought it about. Then on a third, what happened afterwards.

Putting the postcards away, they write in any order those three parts of their story — just one, maybe two paragraphs each, or as little as a line of dialogue.

They then share the results in group discussion to work out how the three parts of the whole story fit together.

-45   DAVID FINE

— WORKSHOP 28 —

Purpose   A simple exercise which develops good dialogue, and helps students to move away from the passive voice.

Materials Enough newspapers to go round.

Method   Ask the class to pick a news story from the paper and write some or all of it as dialogue, as if the reader was there — a bank raid, a shareholders' meeting, Cabinet Minister kiss'n'tell, etc.

They should take care to use the dialogue to convey actions and emotions: 'This is a real gun. Keep calm and do exactly as we tell you...'

-45   DAVID FINE

— WORKSHOP 29 —

Purpose   To freshen up dull writing style, especially with regard to historical fiction, and to encourage factual research.

Materials History books brought by students.

Method   Each student brings along a history book about an event they're interested in. They then write it as if it's happening now, in the present tense, with all reported speech as dialogue. (Remind them, for example, of the Hindenberg disaster.)

-45   DAVID FINE

— WORKSHOP 30 —

Purpose   To lead students, both beginners and others, to the point of having written a poem.

Rationale   Poetry often needs forcing. While one can inspire certain images or ideas by giving students randomly chosen pictures or by playing instrumental music to a class, nothing seems more difficult to unpractised writers of verse than decisions about form. To allow students simply to ramble all over the page in 'free verse' (which they may merely write as chopped-up prose) is likely to be unhelpful.

Any poetry workshop should involve a judicious combination of liberty and restriction — freedom to allow the individual student's imagination to produce what it will, but only within certain strict limitations of form. There does not have to be a clear logic behind the limitations one chooses. Indeed, the quirkier the restrictions the more surprising and imaginative the results.

Method   Different combinations of the following steps may be taken to varying effect:

Randomly read out, (for example) ten unrelated words from a book. Get students to write down the first word that comes to mind in association with each of the ten in turn. Instruct them to write a ten-line text incorporating their ten words, one per line, in the order in which they first noted them down. The topic will dictate itself.

Possible further restrictions:

- allow them to use only (for example) seven words per line.
- specify the first/last word of any particular line(s).
- randomly pick an eleventh word, which they must include in the title of their text.

Between classes, students should rewrite the resulting text to their own satisfaction, perhaps now discarding the given restrictions. At the next class, discuss results. A few will be of little interest. Some will stand as successful short poems on their own; others will look as if they need to be part of something longer. In the latter case, encourage the writer to treat the text as merely one stanza in a longer poem, and to write other stanzas conforming to the same structure (ten lines, seven words to the line, etc.).

Note: initial class reactions to the authoritarian instructions at the start of the exercise are likely to be amused, bewildered and/or irritated. They will think you are mad. (But don't they already?)

-45   GREGORY WOODS

— WORKSHOP 31 —

Purpose   An exercise for students who have recently developed regular writing habits but need to know how best to organise themselves.

Method   Students must get a notebook and use it every time they sit down to write. They should note down:

> The day and date.
> The time they started.
> The time they finished.
> Their mood.
> Where they wrote.
> What they wrote.
> Why they stopped.

After a month, patterns should emerge — how long they can expect to write at one time, when and where they write best, etc.

Group discussion of the diaries can also help to raise issues of time management and motivation.

-45   DAVID FINE

— WORKSHOP 32—

Purpose   To draw attention to ways in which poetic form influences or creates meaning.

Method   Give each student another's poem. Instruct them to rewrite it, but without changing any word or the order in which the words appear. They may only alter line lengths, stanza breaks or other aspects of the words' positions on the page.

Instigate a discussion in which rewriters justify their changes and the original writers comment on the results. How have the changes altered pace, rhythm, tone, meaning?

Note: with access to word processors, students can quickly produce several different versions of a text. They may also choose to experiment with varying typefaces, though some teachers may wish to discourage this.

-45   GREGORY WOODS

— WORKSHOP 33 —

Purpose   Using the five senses in descriptive writing.

Materials   Flashcards.

Method   An emotion or a subject suggested to the students by preparing individual flashcards. Each one must be described using metaphors and similes.

                -15   EDYTH BLOCK

— WORKSHOP 34 —

Purpose   1. To demonstrate the qualities of rhythm.
               2. To practise basic performance skills.

Materials   a) Enough copies for everyone of a sheet featuring a selection of poems, prose, nursery rhymes, technical instructions, etc.

               b) Cassette player and a selection of music e.g. baroque, rap, waltz. Make sure there is a wide selection of speeds and rhythms. (I usually use the sound track from Twin Peaks, some Albinoni, and Push It — an aggressive dance track by Salt'n'Pepa.

Note: always make sure the tapes are pre-set at the desired point before you start. It will spoil the element of surprise if they hear the music beforehand.

Method   Push back the chairs and ask the group to stand in a circle. Talk for a few moments about the importance of performance skills when reading out one's work — posture, voice projection, enunciation, etc.

To get them used to speaking within the circle, go round a few times asking people to count to ten, say the letters of the alphabet, etc. Then begin reading out a poem from the sheet (I use Adrian Henri's *Love Is...*), one line per person, round the circle.

Now it's time for the music. They must read out the poem again, a line each, to the beat of the music — which of course will be changed two or three times. It's an enjoyable non-threatening exercise and soon people will find it hard to keep still! Once they've got the hang of doing this with a fairly clearly rhythmic poem, try them with a non-rhythmic piece, e.g. the instructions for attaching a plug, or a short story extract.

Finally, I like to give students some extra time in pairs to write a special short piece to be performed at the end of the session.

45+   SUE THOMAS

— WORKSHOP 35 —

Purpose   Using the five senses in descriptive writing.

Method   Comparison of locations, e.g. a railway station at rush hour and the same venue at 3 a.m., or a hospital ward contrasting night and day. Start by writing down as many words to these scenes as occur, then fill in the details.

-15   EDYTH BLOCK

— WORKSHOP 36 —

Purpose   To widen our understanding of the short story genre.

Materials   Enough photocopies to go round of the stories below — although it would be possible simply to read them aloud to the class.

Method   Start discussion in groups as to what each student understands by a 'short story'. After the groups have exchanged ideas get each student to list the requirements for a short story.

Read (a) *The Pearl* by Guy de Maupassant, and then without discussion (b) *The Boy* by Joyce Carol Oates.

Ask them to discuss their lists in the light of these two stories in the groups.

After this, hold a plenary discussion on the difficulties of fitting the two stories into their list of requirements.

To push this idea further, read (a) *Love, Your Only Mother* by David Michael Kaplan and then (b) *The Fury* by Stan Barstow.

Get them to discuss the idea further and then send them away to write their own short story, hopefully with a wider perspective on what constitutes a short story.

The Pearl by Guy de Maupassant is easily available in de Maupassant collections in Penguin & Everyman.

The Fury by Stan Barstow is available in *The Desperadoes and other stories* and *The Human Element*, two collections of Stan Barstow stories.

The Boy by Joyce Carol Oates and *Love, Your Only Mother* by David Michael Kaplan are both in *Sudden Fiction International — 60 Short-short Stories* ed. Shepard & Thomas, Paladin, 1991.

45+   BRENDAN MURPHY

— WORKSHOP 37 —

Purpose   Identifying a subject.

Method   A good way to start writing poetry or short stories is to ask yourself to consider the following:

Which experiences will I never forget?

What makes me laugh?

What makes me angry?

Significant dreams.

Who would I like to be?

-15   KENNETH MOOD

— WORKSHOP 38 —

Purpose   Information-giving and narrative.

Materials   A single object or picture.

Method   Using an object or a picture as stimulus, ask questions: who? where? when? why? what?

examples:

Who is in the plot?

Where is this taking place?

Why are these people here?

What has happened/is about to happen?

-15   EDYTH BLOCK

— WORKSHOP 39 —

Purpose   To encourage students to closely examine their surroundings. (This works best when the weather is warm and pleasant!)

Method   **Part One** Send everyone outside with instructions to choose something — an area of grass, or a tree, or an insect, etc. — examine it closely, and then make notes on it. The notes must be as detailed as possible and should be wholly factual. The results can be discussed back in the classroom.

Part Two Ask the class to repeat the previous exercise — but this time they are confined to the classroom.

Encourage them to examine the minutest of details — drawing-pin holes, furniture scratches, etc.

Part Three Readouts and comparisons. I frequently find that students enjoy the second exercise more than the first because it encourages them to look more closely at an everyday environment which is so familiar it has become invisible. There is often a lively discussion about the things we consider worthy of artistic attention, i.e. 'natural' scenes and objects, versus the more mundane features of our physical surroundings.

45+   SUE THOMAS

— WORKSHOP 40 —

Purpose   To free the writer from self-consciousness.

Method   Choose a story that the class knows well, or tell one as baldly as you know how. I have used Greek myths, fairy stories, or urban myths, as a source. Ask the members of the class to re-tell the story in a different setting: for instance, the story of Narcissus can be re-told in contemporary Nottingham, or wartime Berlin, or eighteenth century America, depending upon the individual student's preference. Allow the class to choose any form, any style, any genre they like. I usually ask this to be done as a home assignment to allow the story/poem/drama to be extended as long as is liked, but in the class I should suggest a time of 15-45 minutes.

-45   JACEK LASKOWSKI

— Workshop 41 —

Purpose   To write a poem by committee: based on the pyramid discussion system.

Method   Persuade the group to choose a simple one-word topic for the poem: it can be fun to do this mock-formally with votes, etc. Give out strips of paper, each with a different preposition or initial adverb already written on it. (I usually cut sheets of A4 into eight or ten strips.) Tell the students to write just their one line of the proposed poem, with no other requirement than that it start with the word given. Allow no more than two minutes for this, and include yourself in the task. Ask each to read out their line in turn, slowly.

Then ask for a repeat readaround, telling them to listen out for lines with which they feel their own could go — thematically, stylistically, whatever. Small groups work on putting their individual lines into some sort of order, then look for other groups to whose 'stanza' their own can be juxtaposed. THERE SHOULD NOT BE ANY SIGNIFICANT ADDITIONS OR CUTS TO THE ORIGINAL LINES! Finally, the whole group should be able to perform the 'poem' line by line as an ordered sequence.

30-45 mins, 10-60 students   CATHERINE BYRON

— Workshop 42 —

Purpose   To demonstrate that poetry is neither sacred nor beyond reproach.

Method   Get students to edit canonical poems:

either

give them (say) one of Shakespeare's sonnets and instruct them to render it down to a haiku — assuming
they are already familiar with the latter form;

or

get them to 'translate' a pre-twentieth century poem into
free verse, ironing out its regular metre, removing
rhymes, and substituting contemporary diction for all
archaisms.

Ezra Pound's Imagist rules should be useful here:

a) use no superfluous words;
b) use no ornamentation;
c) use no abstractions.

Discuss the results. What has been lost from the original
poem? Equally important, what has been gained in the
new version? Which do they prefer?

-45   GREGORY WOODS

— WORKSHOP 43 —

Purpose   To increase the students' awareness of visualising some-
              thing and presenting it orally or on paper.

Method   Take students into a clutter-free space which allows for
              freedom of thought.

Spread them out throughout the space and make them stand up with their eyes closed.

Let them move forward, disorientate them, and make them continue standing for a few seconds.

Turn off the light and play a tape containing instrumental music.

They will start to feel a range of different sensations, based on the scenario you create in their mind, e.g. a piece of creepy music could symbolise a haunted house.

Once the music has finished, turn on the lights and tell them to open their eyes.

Get them to write down immediately what they saw in their minds, what they felt, and any other sensations which were taking place. This becomes the first draft.

Once the first draft is completed get them to look at:

a) the structure
b) the language
c) the order

Get them to look at ways of improving the piece. Inform them that they are going through a process called editing.

Once they have completed the second draft let them read it out to the same piece of music, to experience the effect of reading to the music which gave birth to the original idea. This will enable you to deal with issues of diction, language acquisition and presentation skills.

Note: students who can't write should dictate it to those who can transcribe it for them.

Listening to music 5 mins

1st draft 30/40 mins

Discussion 15/20 mins

2nd draft 30/40 mins

Evaluation 15/20 mins   MARTIN GLYNN

— WORKSHOP 44 —

Purpose   A beginner's exercise designed to isolate some basic elements within linear storytelling. NOT to be used as a method for telling a story. To identify strengths and weaknesses in creative writing.

Method   1. Describe a place/location and make it appeal to all the senses. Help your reader to see it, smell it, touch it, hear it, taste it. Remember, your location does not have to be naturalistic.

   2. Introduce three or four characters into the place without using dialogue.

   3. Introduce dialogue between some or all of the characters.

   4. Optional: develop the plot into a full story.

   up to one hour   KEVIN FEGAN

— WORKSHOP 45 —

Purpose   To provide science fiction-based ideas for stories and poems.

Method   *either*

Ask students to each provide a 'what-if' for the central pool. They can then draw out ideas at random and develop them.

or

Provide the ideas yourself. For example:

What if...

... the sun only shone for one hour a day?

... all women/men had a telepathic twin?

... for one day only, you could teleport yourself anywhere instantly?

... you had the power of flight/invisibility/shape-shifting

... you were allowed to ask just one question a day, which constitutes your only education?

... human beings are merely the second most intelligent species on the planet, and must suffer the consequences of being dominated by the master species (which is...?).

... as you become older, you shrink in size at a rate of one inch per year.

... power and prestige accrue in direct response to one's degree of ruthlessness and maliciousness.

... one each day, people with dark hair (e.g.) can leap forward five minutes in time at a moment of their choosing, rearrange the near-future, then leap back.

-45   STEVE BOWKETT

— WORKSHOP 46 —

Purpose   An opportunity for people to get to know each other and share ideas.

Method   Ask students to sit quietly and think of one question they'd like to ask all other group members (one question each, same question to be asked of everyone else in the group). The question should be geared towards the mutual interest and preoccupation of the group, i.e. writing. Try to avoid obvious ones like 'who's your favourite author?'

Give everyone the chance to move around the room and interview each other with the one question each. (Answers should be recorded.) This can take a long time. Rather than set an end point it is worth checking now and again how far people have got and encouraging any 'slowies' to hurry along.

When all interviews are complete, ask people to team up in pairs to assess their findings with a view to presenting them to the group either verbally or on a large sheet of paper (if available).

45+   BARRY WAKEFIELD

— WORKSHOP 47 —

Purpose To demonstrate the way in which a feature article may be written.

Materials Enough copies of a selected newspaper article to go round, or a selection of different articles.

Method Ask the students to read the article carefully, and then use a separate sheet to answer the following questions:

- Who would read this article?

- List and identify the different sources used.

- Which questions do you think the reporter asked?

- How much of the piece is direct quotation, and how much is the reporter's own words?

- What other research material could have been used?

After a plenary session drawing together their findings, ask them to rework the piece in one of a variety of ways, e.g.:

- Recycle this information to fit a very different publication, e.g. *The Sun; Cosmopolitan; The Independent,* etc.

- Rewrite, cutting the number of words in half.

- Rewrite as fiction; as poetry; as an item for radio.

45+   SUE THOMAS

— WORKSHOP 48 —

Purpose   To develop dialogue.

Method   Divide students into groups and give them a general topic or narrative situation from which to construct a scene in dialogue. This can be made more or less specific, or different groups can be given slightly different tasks, e.g. some can be asked to create dialogue in the style of soap opera, others in the style of other particular genres (or particular dramatists, etc.)

-45   JANETTE DILLON

3.7 Workshop exercises with accompanying handouts

The following set of exercises is designed as a skeleton framework for tutors wishing to provide technical information. Each one has its own accompanying copyright-free handout at the end of the section.

Important   These exercises and handouts, like all of the suggestions in this book, have been devised in order to support tutors in training.

- Each handout is not designed to stand alone, but should be used in conjunction with the appropriate teaching session.

- These handouts and exercises are offered as a simple foundation for development, and should be tailored to suit each tutor's own personalised methods and resources.

- The handouts may also be used as a basis for designing further teaching aids.

- There are no timings provided in this section. As a rough guide, each exercise will probably take up a whole session, sometimes two, and some need prior preparatory input.

- You can devise more of these handouts yourself. Further topics could include: poetic forms and styles; script layouts; research techniques, etc.

— HANDOUT TOPICS —

The Main Components of Fiction (pages 108-109)

Creating Fiction (page110)

Building a Character (page 111)

Editing and Revision (pages 112-113)

Submitting Work for Publication (pages 114-115)

Studying a Novel: *The French Lieutenant's Woman* (page 116)

Some Common Word Processing Mistakes (page 117)

Each handout is free of copyright and may be reproduced for teaching purposes.

— WORKSHOP WITH HANDOUT 1 —

Handout   MAIN COMPONENTS OF FICTION (pages 108-109)

Purpose   To provide a theoretical background to fiction-writing. Also gives a vocabulary for students to use when discussing their own and each others' work.

Materials   Copies of the handout above.

Method   Lead the students through the handout, explaining as you go. Some of the ideas may be very new and difficult to grasp at first (e.g. the concept of 'plot' as being different from 'story') so proceed slowly until you're sure that everyone understands the handout.

Follow-up   Follow this exercise, either for the rest of this session or during the next, with CREATING FICTION.

— WORKSHOP WITH HANDOUT 2 —

Handout   CREATING FICTION (page 110)

Purpose   To allow students to put into practice the concepts they learned from MAIN COMPONENTS OF FICTION. On this occasion the group uses the story provided, but they should subsequently be encouraged to analyse their own and each other's work.

Materials   Copies of the handout and copies of a published short story.

Note: choose this story carefully, making sure that it provides plenty of material for discussion.

Method

- Distribute the copies of the story, then read it aloud to the group. (You might like to practice this beforehand.)

- Ask them to jot down quickly what they remember most from the story, and what they think it's about.

- Divide the group into pairs or threes and ask them to compare notes for a minute or two.

- Distribute the handout CREATING FICTION and explain it — at the same time refreshing their memories of the categories described in MAIN COMPONENTS OF FICTION.

- Divide the questions up between the groups. Remember that you don't have to stick rigidly to the list on the sheet. You might like, for example, to give each group one question and questions 8, 9 and 10, and then keep some other questions aside for the group to discuss. Or, of course, you could omit some. E.g.:

  Group A to discuss question 1 + 8, 9, 10

Group B	"	2	"
Group C	"	3	"
Group D	"	4	"

  Whole group to discuss questions 5, 6 and 7 later in the session.

- Each group can now appoint a scribe to make notes and report back at the plenary, and then begin to discuss their allotted topics.

- Plenary. Explain that dividing up the questions this way speeds up understanding, as each group is working for the benefit and enlightenment of the whole, but it's important to be concise. Each group (either together or through their scribe) should now report back on their single question. Don't allow them to proceed to 8, 9 and 10 because you will cover those afterwards. Some discussion can be allowed, but keep a close watch on the time or you may find yourself beaten by the clock.

- After each has reported on their single question you can discuss 8, 9 and 10 as a whole group.

Note

This type of discussion-based learning covers the most ground when it's kept under extremely tight control — it can easily become rambling and time-consuming. The tutor should, whilst circulating amongst the groups, steer conversations towards the more productive areas. And watch the clock. Lengthy, rambling chats may be enjoyable but the purpose of this exercise is to measurably advance the students' understanding. Make sure you leave yourself 5-10 minutes before the end to recap the evening's work with particular stress on the way it will help the students to talk about their own writing.

— WORKSHOP WITH HANDOUT 3 —

Handout   BUILDING A CHARACTER (page 111)

Purpose   To expand upon characters the students have already created, and to give them confidence in their own powers of imagination.

Materials   Copies of the handout.

Method   *either*

ask the students to think about a character they have previously written about,

or

give them a short writing exercise to develop a character. (One of the -15 exercises in this pack would do very well.)

- Explain that these 'imaginary' people are perhaps much more alive than we might think. This exercise is designed not to invent, but to release information which already exists.

- Distribute the handouts and tell them to answer the questions on the sheet by writing down the first answers to come into their heads. They should not worry if the answers seem mundane or uninteresting. Just write them down as they come.

Rule: even if your character is really you (and how many aren't?), it is vital that you think and write your answers in the 3rd person.

- Plenary. Students discuss their results in small groups, or all together. Ask them to explain how the exercise has revealed new ideas and pathways for the story.

— WORKSHOP WITH HANDOUT 4 —

Handout   EDITING and REVISION (pages 112-113)

Purpose   To help develop critical and editorial skills.

Materials   Copies of the students' own writing + edited mss and proofs if available.

HEALTH WARNING Students must understand that 'perfected' pieces are not suitable for this workshop. It is designed to provide careful, honest and rigorous feedback.

Method   *At least one week ahead*

Ask everyone to photocopy a piece of writing they feel could use some feedback. This workshop is not suitable for original copies, or for showing off work the writer feels is already perfect!

On the day

Explain the work of professional editors, especially stressing the fact that very few authors are published without being edited first. Explain that the function of an editor is not to cause pain (!) but to bring out the best in a writer.

Use the handout to discuss the sorts of problems the students will be looking for.

Tell the students to decide what they would like to know about the piece they are submitting for criticism, and ask them to jot down their questions at the top of Page One. This could be asking for help with spelling and punctuation, or requesting an initial emotional response to the work.

After a final reminder that positive encouragement is also valuable, students can now begin to swap their work with each other, and get down to the actual hard work of critiquing and annotating the writing. The tutor can keep this going by being on hand to pass work around.

End with a discussion about what they have learned about both giving and receiving criticism.

— WORKSHOP WITH HANDOUT 5 —

Handout   SUBMITTING WORK FOR PUBLICATION
(pages 114-115)

Purpose   To help students prepare their work for submission to editors, and to give them an insight into the world of publishing.

Materials   Copies of the handout plus any or all of the following if available:

- sample copies of reference works like *The Writer's and Artist's Yearbook, The Writer's Handbook,* etc.

- samples of how to present (and how not to present!) a manuscript.

- sample copies of typescripts, page-proofs, jacket proofs, drama, TV and radio scripts, etc.

- samples of covering letters to editors.

- newspaper articles, etc. featuring interviews with editors and agents.

Method
This session is generally quite information-based, and relies heavily on the tutor's own knowledge and fields of expertise. You should at least ensure that you cover the following topics:

- the range of markets available.

- the importance of finding the most appropriate publisher/magazine for your work.

- how to prepare a manuscript for submission.

- how to write a covering letter.

- the importance of understanding an editor's/agent's point of view, and what their involvement means.

- copyright law in terms of a) the author's own writing and b) use of quotes, lyrics, visuals, etc. from other people's work.

- DON'T FORGET TO INCLUDE a discussion on strategies for coping with rejection.

Note
Your students will have stories to tell about their brushes with the publishing world, so make sure you use that resource too.

— WORKSHOP WITH HANDOUT 6 —

Handout   STUDYING A NOVEL: *The French Lieutenant's Woman* (page 116)

Purpose   For students who are reluctant readers, or who are unfamiliar with literary study.

Materials   Copies of the handout + the class should all have read *The French Lieutenant's Woman* by John Fowles, and should have their copies with them.

Method   *One month beforehand:*

The class: make sure that everyone has a copy of the novel and give them a deadline by which to have read it.

The tutor: supplement your own reading of the novel by reading some background information and literary criticism. You should also work through the handout yourself so that you have some answers ready if necessary.

On the day:

Give a short talk on the importance of readers being writers too. (You may prefer to cover this in an earlier session.)

Introduce the novel with a short mini-lecture which you have prepared from your own research (above).

Talk the class through the handout, explaining what each question means, then simply work through it either in small groups (see the workshop on CREATING FICTION) or together.

Variations   a) Use any novel and prepare your own handout.

b) You may find it easier to visit your local bookshop and browse through the literature study guides. You can choose a title from there, and use a GCSE or A Level study guide to prepare your own worksheet and 'mini-lecture'.

— WORKSHOP WITH HANDOUT 7 —

Handout   SOME COMMON WORD PROCESSING MISTAKES
               (page 117)

Purpose   A trouble-shooting session designed to open up problems of a general nature as well as word processing.

Materials   Copies of the handout

               + copies of a poem or story with the punctuation and capitals removed

               + samples of general problem pieces (spelling, punctuation, syntax, etc.).

Method   Encourage people to talk about their own problems with spelling, etc. and discuss ways in which they can improve and learn.

               Distribute copies of the poem or story without punctuation and ask the students, either alone or in pairs, to put in the punctuation. You could also distribute other examples if you have them.

               Then bring the group together and discuss the results.

106

Distribute copies of the word processing handout and explain it. This might lead to a discussion on how students actually do their writing, e.g.: by hand, directly onto the screen, sitting at a desk, lying on the floor, etc. and the merits of these various approaches.

Note: since this is a trouble-shooting session it can go off in any direction, but make sure you keep notes so that you can sum up at the end.

Main Components of Fiction - 1

(developed from 'Aspects of the Novel', E.M. Forster)

Story   is based on the simple storyteller — a teller and an audience. A narrative of events arranged in their time-sequence.

Plot   is a narrative of events with the emphasis falling on causality. THE KING DIED AND THEN THE QUEEN DIED is a story, but THE KING DIED AND THEN THE QUEEN DIED OF GRIEF is a plot because it makes us ask why? and how? It feeds our curiosity, our intelligence and our powers of memory.

Characters can be used to thread in and out as needed, but the main difference between fictional characters and real people is that, if the author so desires, we can know a lot about their internal worlds and their life history. This seldom occurs even with those you know and love best in real life.

Flat and Rounded Characters have different functions:-

FLAT are useful for the plot. They are predictable and uncomplicated. Best used for humour/crime/romance.

ROUNDED are more complex. Perhaps the story hinges on their own self-discovery, or maybe they're used to test out a situation.

Main Components of Fiction - 2

Pattern makes the shape of the narrative — linear, circular, twisting, etc.

Rhythm makes the music of the narrative — perhaps in repeated and elaborated phrases of imagery.

Hooks persuade the reader to turn the page and read on. These work on a much lower level than plot, and can be very simple indeed. Eg:

- when a telephone rings, we want to know who's calling.
- when a character is afraid of spiders, we want them to encounter one.
- when a character desires something — a lover, a new hat, a buttered scone — we want to see them get/not get it.
- when the reader knows something the character doesn't know (there is a rabid dog around the next corner) we expect there to be an outcome or meeting of some kind. The dog can't just wander off in the opposite direction, as might happen in Real Life.

Hooks can work the other way around, too. If you're having trouble with a character make them want something and then send them chasing after it...

Creating Fiction

Read the story carefully, then answer the following questions:

1. Identify the story of the story by listing the events in the order in which they are given. (Remember that 'story' is different to 'plot'.)

2. Identify the plot of the story.

3. Make a list of all the people who appear in the story, then divide them into 'round' and 'flat' characters. Give reasons for each of your decisions.

4. List all the hooks you can find, both large and small. How do they work?

5. Look at the story in terms of pattern and rhythm. Can you make a drawing of these shapes?

6. What is the time order of the narrative?

7. What is the narrator's involvement in the story?

8. What did you enjoy most about the story?

9. What did you enjoy least?

10. Has this story given you any new ideas to try out in your own writing?

Building a Character

When I'm writing anovel, I'm dealing with a double life. I live in the present at the same time that I live in the past with my characters.

John Philips Marquand

This exercise is designed to expand upon a character you've already created. You may not eventually use all of the information below, but it should help to clarify your ideas. Answer the following questions as quickly as possible and without too much deliberation.

Rule: Write about this character in the 3rd person — do not allow yourself to slip into a 1st person narrative!

1. Write down two random facts about this person.
2. What is their most important life event to date?
3. If they could change one thing about their life so far, what would it be?
4. Who do they love?
5. Who do they hate?
6. What is their favourite item of clothing?
7. How do they envisage their life ten years from now?
8. What makes them angry?
9. What frightens them?
10. What thrills them?
11. What is their earliest childhood memory?
12. What do they want more than anything in the world?
13. Is this a secret or a public desire?
14. What does their voice sound like?
15. What is the texture of their skin?

Editing and Revision - 1

The process of making art can be broken down into three main stages. Stages 1 and 2 may add up to as little as a few hours, whereas Stage 3 could last for years.

Stage 1: The idea

This may be a response to outer or inner stimuli — perhaps as fleeting as a face seen in a crowd, or a remembered fragrance.

Stage 2 : Working it through

This is your initial written response to the idea: the first draft. This stage of the process often plots a messy and chaotic path which you must follow in order to refine your thoughts.

Stage 3: Evaluation and revision

After a period of time (hours, days, weeks) a coherent structure begins to rise from the first raw drafts.

Getting feedback

It's difficult to get honest honest opinions about your writing. Family and friends will want to boost your confidence by admiring everything you do, whilst non-readers may not understand what you're trying to achieve.

Of course, what you really need is a sympathetic professional editor, but for the moment you must learn the skill yourself. The best way to do this is to edit other people's work, and to have them edit you. Many of us are afraid to be truthful, fearing that we will damage the budding writer, but feedback is vital if one is to improve.

As a rule of thumb, try to find at least *one good thing* and *one bad thing* to say about the work.

Editing and Revision - 2

The job of an editor

The function of an editor is to bring out the best in a writer. Very few authors are published without some editorial input. Indeed, when a writer feels too important to take notice of editorial advice the effect will quickly begin to show.

What to look for

*   Where does the piece actually start?
*   Do you find the piece convincing?
*   Is any of it — unnecessary? irrelevant? repetitious?
*   Are there any problems with spelling? punctuation? grammar?
*   Do the sentences and paragraphs flow easily?
*   Is it too wordy, too minimal or too inhibited?
*   Is the structure appropriate?
*   Is the writing too obviously derivative of another author's style?
*   Does the piece have a satisfying ending/conclusion?
*   Would the piece benefit from more specific description?
*   Do you believe in the characters?
*   Does the dialogue sound natural?
*   Is it well-researched?
*   Can you identify the audience for this piece?
*   Does it communicate successfully to its intended audience?
*   Is it of the right length and complexity?
*   Is it rhythmically satisfying?

and of course:

*   Which parts of it do you *really love*?
*   Which parts move you to tears, or make you laugh, or mirror something in your own experience?
*   Remember — even the worst writing will contain something to be commended.

Submitting Work for Publication - 1

Presentation of manuscripts

* Submissions should *always* be type-written and double-spaced.
* Use one side of the paper only.
* Margins: (min.) left 2"; right 1"; top and bottom 1".
* Number your pages.
* Each page should carry your name and the title of the piece.
* The whole should carry a front-sheet with your name, address, title of piece, approx. word-length, and a copyright statement, e.g. 'Copyright J. Bloggs 1993'.
* Do not staple your work — a paper-clip is better.
* For lengthy mss., e.g. a novel, place typescript in *loose-leaf* form inside a folder. Plastic binders are difficult to access and often obscure the left side of the page.
* Always enclose an s.a.e. for return of your ms.
* Send three poems at a time to give the editor a fair idea of your style. Stories, however, are usually submitted singly.

Payment

Extremely variable, from nothing upwards. See *The Writer's Handbook* or *The Writers' & Artists' Yearbook* for current rates plus listings of the huge variety of poetry, fiction & non-fiction publishers, markets, and awards. Just don't expect to get rich.

Research your market

Give preference to magazines you already enjoy and feel in tune with. What is the average length of the stories/poems they already publish? What are they about? Send your work to a named editor — often found at the front of the magazine — otherwise, phone and ask who you should submit to. You might like to check whether they are looking at work at the moment

Submitting Work for Publication - 2

Rejections

Everyone gets them! If you receive more than a standard reply, think yourself lucky and take note of the editor's comments. You may or may not agree; you may decide you'd chosen the wrong magazine; you may wish to re-write it if the editor has asked you to. And editors can make mistakes...

Small press magazines

Usually only available by postal subscription. Their editors are often interested in new writers and may even take the time to give you a short crit but it's *vital* that you read a magazine first to find out if it's for you. There are dozens to choose from, but here are a few to try:

CASCANDO Publishes writers who are students. Cascando Press Ltd, P.O. Box 1499, London SW10 9TZ.

IRON Interested in new writers. Ed. Peter Mortimer, 5 Marden Terrace, Cullercoats, North Shields, Tyne & Wear NE30 4PD.

LONDON MAGAZINE Ed. Alan Ross, 30 Thurloe Place, London SW7.

PANURGE Interested in new writers. Ed. John Murray. Crooked Holme Farm Cottage, Brampton, Cumbria CA8 2AT.

STAND Jon Silkin, 179 Wingrove Road, Newcastle-upon-Tyne NE4 9DA.

WRITING WOMEN Women only. Ed. Eileen Aird + 3 others. 10 Mistletoe Road, Newcastle-upon-Tyne NE2 2DX.

NB: Small presses are always short of money. Subscribe if you can.

Studying a Novel:
The French Lieutenant's Woman by John Fowles

The historical novel

1. Define an 'historical novel' in thirty words or less.

2. List the historical novels you have read. Do they conform to the definition you've given above?

3. Is *The French Lieutenant's Woman* a historical novel? Why? Why not?

The French Lieutenant's Woman

1. Chapter 3 begins by apparently breaking some of the cardinal rules of historical fiction. Can you identify these irregularities?

2. Why do you think John Fowles used the quotation about President Kennedy at the beginning of Chapter 20? What effect does it have upon the reader?

3. The novel seems to reach a conclusive finish at the end of Chapter 44, then changes tack and begins again. Did this please you? Why? Why not? Which ending do you prefer? Why?

4. Read Chapter 55. How do you respond to it *as a reader*?

Your own writing...

1. Read Chapter 55. How do you respond to it *as a writer*?

2. List the problems you have encountered when writing about a real or fictional past.

3. Has this novel prompted you to approach your own writing differently? If so, how?

Some Common Word Processing Mistakes

At first glance, a word-processed document always looks more efficient and professional than one which has been hand-written, and tidier than a type-written document spotted with correction fluid. However, many people bring their stylistic errors to the computer, making it more difficult to operate a spell-check and reducing the readability of the document. Here are some tips to improve the quality of your documents:

1. *Punctuation* should not be placed like this,because not only does this practice link words together(confusing the spell-checker)but it also tightens up the appearance of the text,making it difficult to read. So make sure that you leave a space after **,;:**. But there are exceptions to this rule, for example:

   > HYPHENS Report-writing.
   >
   > APOSTROPHES Jane's hat.
   >
   > SPEECH-MARKS She said "It's Jane's hat".
   >
   > PARENTHESES Space before (first and after last) bracket

3. Make hood use of tour **spell-checker**, but be aware that errors resulting in at alternative 'proper ward' will not be picked up. There it stilt a need for visual checking.

4. *You will probably have a choice of* **fonts** on your software. Use **bold**, ^{super}script, and $_{sub}$script to good effect,but always run a trial print-out.

5. Make sure you set your **page-length** correctly, so that your text does not run onto the next sheet without a break.

6. Turn OFF the right-justification — a ragged right-hand margin makes reading easier.

7. And don't forget to turn page-numbers ON.

Writers
on
Teaching

JACEK LASKOWSKI

I fell into teaching creative writing by chance. Indeed, if someone had asked me at the beginning whether or not I believed that creative writing was something that could be taught, I would probably have said I did not. Now, ten years later, I am occasionally asked how many of my students, of whom there have been several hundred, have written best-sellers. I admit that, as far as I know, none have. In addition, again only as far as I know, Jeffrey Archer, Danielle Steele, Catherine Cookson and Jackie Collins all have in common the fact that they did not attend any creative writing courses before they became millionaires and once they had become millionaires none of them was tempted to take one. Consequently, creative writing is a singular waste of time. Q.E.D.

Over the years, a proportion of participants at my courses has been haunted by the spectre of best-sellerdom. Usually most of the haunted ones leave when it transpires, as it rapidly does, that there is no guarantee of commercial or critical success even after eighteen ninety-minute meetings with me and the other members of the course. Once or twice a haunted one has completed the course with religious scrupulousness and growing frustration, until he or she could stand it no more. Then all the disappointment was poured into a vituperative letter attacking me for anything from incompetence to megalomania. I have had one letter lambasting me for everything from incompetence to megalomania; it finished with an attack on the writer's fellow participants' stupidity, lack of talent, and aesthetic idiocy.

Fortunately, these outbursts are rare. That they happen is partly the tutor's fault in that he has clearly not answered a need. Partly, however, it is also due to the vagueness of the concept of creative writing, a vagueness which permits people to join the courses in the not entirely reasonable anticipation that they will be instructed in eighteen, or twelve, or even fewer easy lessons how to make big money with their pens (and it is usually pens we are dealing with here, not typewriters or word processors). As one of my students put it: 'If he (meaning me) knew how to write a best-seller, he wouldn't be sitting here talking to us lot on a wet winter Thursday in Matlock'.

Of course it's not possible to teach anyone how to write a best-seller simply because the definition of a best-seller is that it sells millions of copies, and over that no tutor can have any influence. What can be taught is how to write Mills and Boon type books, how to write detective novels, historical novels, thrillers, chillers, sci-fi and humorous books. There are numerous handbooks setting out, in considerable detail, how to set about constructing this kind of novel, or that kind of television play. There are, furthermore, courses which deal with the same subjects. The Arvon Foundation courses are the best known and, by and large, probably the best, too, in dealing with specific genres as well as more general topics.

But creative writing courses are different. It took me some time to find this out, and before I did find out I probably laboured under a similar misapprehension as had my haunted friends. I think that for a while I probably did imagine that the measure of my success would be the number of published writers that would graduate from the course. Some have been published, true. But the greatest teaching triumphs have not necessarily come from the publication of a story or a poem: they have come from helping the participants of the courses to find their own voices.

The voice I am talking about is the way in which an individual recounts the experiences, feelings, imagined events, or thoughts that are important to him or her. The teaching of English in schools, with its prescriptive dogmatism, its emphasis on analysis and criticism, its insistence on imposing hierarchies of values, has managed to deprive many people, especially those who are now elderly, of the most natural means of self-expression: expression through language. Nowadays, English is taught with more sensitivity, more attention is paid to ways in which an individual can use language to express his or her own creative aspirations. Nevertheless, much damage is still being done by making children (and children grow into self-conscious adults) compare their own work unfavourably with the writings of the good and the great, with the literary masterpieces of Austen or Dickens, Hemingway or Conrad, Salinger or Golding. Or even with the best-sellers of Archer and Steele. Because they have been compared unfavourably, many individual voices have been muted, often silenced permanently. It is very often, I would say in my experience predominantly, the job of the creative writing tutor to help his students to recover that voice, to make them recognise it as their own, and to help them acknowledge that it is valuable.

Why is it valuable? Not because it will help to create a best-seller, though it may do that, too. It is valuable because an ability to express oneself allows one to communicate more fully with others, to communicate more profoundly with oneself, to appreciate that one's experiences, thoughts, imagined events, feelings have a meaning outside themselves. If one has a voice, one can, literally, create something out of nothing.

That is what I have come to realise about the role of the creative writing class. I have been helped in coming to this realisation by many people, most of them students at my courses, the stroppy no less than the enthusiastic acolytes who have, occasionally, blossomed extraordinarily. I have been helped, too, by many writers on the subject of writing, two of whom have been profoundly influential. Dorothea Brande wrote the wisest and best practical book on writing I have come across. It's called *Becoming a Writer* and is essential material for any creative writing tutor. The other book I have found more useful than most in combating despair or disillusion, my own and that of my students, is Victoria Nelson's *Writer's Block and How to Use It* (a typically American, upbeat title), published by World's Digest Books. I recommend it warmly.

After some ten years of teaching creative writing at adult education evening classes and at various residential courses, I still don't know if creative writing can be taught. What I think I know is that with a little enthusiasm, a little faith, and lots of patience we tutors can, from time to time, hear people find ways of expressing themselves. And that can be just as rewarding as seeing their names in print.

Jacek Laskowski was born in Edinburgh and brought up in London. He studied at Cambridge, Krakow, and St Andrews. He is a playwright, a translator (from Polish, French, Russian and Czech), and a storyteller, as well as a creative writing tutor for the WEA/University of Nottingham and a drama tutor at the Arvon Foundation. His most recent production was the acclaimed version of Molière's *Wiseguy Scapino* for Theatr Clwyd.

4. Problems and Issues

4.1 Agony column

Q. *I plan my sessions down to the minute, but still either run out of material too soon or end up rushing through to get it all finished.*

A. Some new tutors give the group too much material, then hurry them through it too fast, whilst others arrive with too little to do. Try to prepare work with plenty of natural breaks so that it can be continued the following week if necessary. It's more important that everyone gets enough time to write and the chance to speak. It's also useful to have at hand a few discussion topics and filler items.

Q. *My students are so obsessed with getting published that the work they produce is mediocre and derivative. They're always talking about markets and copyright law instead of about writing.*

A. In some cases the yearning to be published can act as a real block and students who concentrate on fulfilling what they see to be the requirements of a particular market often forget to enjoy themselves. Such groups can foster a strong and destructive atmosphere of competition, but there's no easy way to dislodge this obsession.

Disentangling students' self-esteem from their publication record is a lengthy and emotional process, but perhaps you could start by promoting honest discussion about the issue and what drives it. Try, too, taking them back to basic stimulus exercises, and get them talking about their private desire to write.

Q. Every week our sessions are ruined by a student who constantly interrupts and dominates the conversation.

A. Interrupters are often driven by enthusiasm but can become a real irritation if not controlled. Try holding all discussions in the round, and in severe cases, adopt the 'tennis-ball rule' where only the holder of the tennis-ball may speak.

Q. One student attends every week, but never joins in and always sits alone during coffee-break.

A. Sometimes a student seems to set themselves apart from the group. Most often this is due to shyness and sometimes a little gentle cajoling is all that's needed.

But occasionally the problem is more severe. When addressed their replies may seem inconsequential and detached, or they may never join in at all. There could be several reasons for this. Check for a hearing disability, a literacy problem, or psychiatric illness.

Q. *I have a student who always keeps me talking after a session. I feel pursued by them but can't say 'no'.*

A. Some students are very needy and will bring you extra work to read or regularly ask for a private chat after the session. The group atmosphere is not enough for them — they want your undivided attention. This may be for their writing or for their personal problems. Be assertive (see Section 4.5).

Q. *I feel constantly inferior to the people I'm teaching. Some of them have published much more than I have.*

A. Just because they're published doesn't mean there's nothing left to learn, and some writers simply enjoy mixing with others and working in a group. They must be getting something out of it. You could, of course, ask them what it is... or why not just assume they like your group and take it as a compliment?

4.2 Racism, sexism, eurocentrism and other oppressions

A random spot-check of writers' groups in the East Midlands produced the following statistics: out of 123 students surveyed, 72 were women and 51 were men. Of those 123, 122 were white. And over two-thirds were retired. It seems therefore safe to assume that the archetypal member of a writer's group is a white female pensioner. Why should this be? Where are the black writers? The young? The lesbian and gay?

It appears that most writers' groups are trapped inside a bubble of elderly, white, probably heterosexual, female British culture. Not only does this bubble exclude young non-white homosexual men and women, but it also secludes and protects those within it. And yet creative writing can transform racism and bigotry through the enlargement of imagination and sympathies and also through the growth of self-esteem.

This can be done effectively through writing exercises based around the principle of 'otherness' in which students are asked to identify with characters utterly different from themselves: physically, morally, intellectually, perhaps in gender or age or privilege. Such exercises aim to liberate writers from narrow and narcissistic viewpoints and to excite them with a sense of the many voices available to them.

Tutors should ensure that the examples of writing they use in class, and the stories and novels they discuss, reflect a wide range of cultural diversity, and they should also be aware of the ways in which eurocentrism influences British cultural perspectives.

Dealing with oppressions within the group

Women encounter particular problems since male students have a reputation for playing topdoggery by constantly challenging and undermining other members of the group. And a frequent problem which most tutors have encountered is knowing how to deal with the writing of pornography. Many women find it difficult to challenge the authors of upsetting and offensive material, and the tutor must have a policy for handling this situation when it arises.

Most writing tutors develop their own methods and sixth sense for coping with incidents of racism, sexism, classism, etc. within the group. Knowing when to deflect an offensive comment with a gentle joke or disassociation, and when to take a stand and directly confront the perpetrator seems to be a matter of courage, resourcefulness and judgement.

Indeed, our society seems to assume that women have a responsibility to educate men; that lesbians and gay men should educate the heterosexual world; that the physically disabled should educate the able-bodied, etc. But this is relieving the oppressors, since that is what they often are, from any responsibility to educate themselves. Tutors wishing to address the roots of oppression in their workshops may find it useful to approach the task from the point of view of identifying that tiny part of the oppressor which is resident inside each of us, be we oppressor or oppressed.

Staffing can be a problem, since the tutors themselves generally do not reflect a wide range of cultural diversity. Perhaps if this issue is firmly addressed it will help to combat the present insularity of existing groups.

Many writers resist being categorised in any way at all, but some groups might wish to experiment with a deliberately exclusive membership — all-lesbian, or all-black, or all under-25, etc.

4.3 Writing as therapy

Opinions about using writing as a therapeutic tool differ widely. Some tutors use it as an ongoing and integral part of their teaching; others use it occasionally; still others feel passionately that art and therapy do not mix under any circumstances. There are also, of course, wide differences between those authors who consider all of their own writing to be therapeutic, and those who divide their work into 'therapy' and 'art', and tend to value the second more than the first.

Maybe it all comes back to the question of why we write in the first place — is it a desire to communicate, or perhaps a form of catharsis to purge and soothe our aching souls? Some teachers and students say that the important thing is to 'write it all down and get it out', thus confronting and working through vital personal issues, whilst others insist that the author must remain distant and detached from the text.

Some groups undeniably have a therapeutic focus. In recent years there have been a number of writers-in-residence in prisons, hospices, high-security and long-term psychiatric hospitals, and this practice seems likely to continue. Added to this, the Education Departments within many prisons run classes in creative writing, and there is also an increasing range of both short-term and long-term community-based residencies working with people who have mental health problems, physical disabilities or learning difficulties.

Because of the variety implicit in such individually-tailored placements it's almost impossible to generalise about 'writing as therapy', and there is continuing and passionate debate amongst the artistic community regarding the nature of the difference, if indeed there is one, between 'therapeutic art' and 'non-therapeutic art'.

There are definitely, however, certain clear distinctions in terms of the practical organisation of writers' groups working inside special institutions, where even the simplest act becomes complex and encircled by artificial limitations. Writers can quickly become valued and trusted by prisoners and patients as non-judgemental and non-institutionalised outsiders, but unfortunately this is sometimes counteracted by the mistrust and resentment of the staff. On occasions it seems impossible to please both sides, yet if writers are to get the most out of a residency this is what they must try to do.

It's clear that a writer working within an institution should remain alert to the nature of the system within which they have to operate. They must think carefully about boundaries. How far should they keep to the rules, and how far should they flout them? Do they have a good sense of the limits of their own privacy and personal space, and are they sensitive to those of the students? Even the very material which makes up the contents of the writer's 'tool-bag' may have to be adapted for a therapeutic environment, as the most innocuous writing exercise can key into some past or present trauma. Tutors must always be conscious of their power and influence, and use it sensitively and with responsibility.

Tutors who work with writing as therapy need very specialised support, and often find that they can relate to inmates and employees of their institution more easily than other writing professionals working in less therapeutic environments. It's vital that such tutors are given the opportunity to come together to discuss and share their very particular problems and approaches.

4.4 Group dynamics and class interactions

Formal and informal evaluations can help students to express their conscious feelings and opinions. But sometimes, and for no apparent reason, nothing seems to gel and the group appears to be in serious danger of falling apart. However all may not be lost because you might be able to retrieve the situation through a judicious examination of the unspoken interactions going on between the people involved.

Read up on interpersonal relationships and try to observe the way your students interact. It's very useful to develop a sixth sense in terms of your awareness to group dynamics so that problems can be nipped in the bud as soon as they arise. Try to observe the interactions at work within the group. They will be operating on a series of different levels:

Features to look for

Atmosphere	Does everyone appear relaxed and comfortable?
Listening	Is it happening?
Participation	Does everyone make an equal contribution?
Criticism	How is it given and taken?

Disagreement   How does the group handle this when it arises?

Awareness   Are participants sensitive to each other's needs?

Dominance   Is the group dominated by a few students?

Repetition   Do some people keep saying the same thing over and over?

Involvement   Have some students clearly switched-off and excluded themselves?

Body language

When we meet someone new we've generally made up our minds about them before they've even said a word. Body language, or non-verbal communication, is extraordinarily powerful. To find out how your students interact, observe the amount of eye contact going on, and between whom. Who avoids eye contact altogether? How are they sitting? Are their bodies turned away from, or towards, each other? Are students sitting in an open position, or are they huddled up with arms folded? A person who keeps a hand over their mouth is probably resisting the urge to speak. Look for mirroring. People who feel in accord tend to unconsciously copy each other's gestures — the sip of coffee, the fiddling with the hair.

What are you saying with *your* body language? When a new group first meets, everyone is nervous, but the tutor has the benefit of invested authority. Make sure you smile often to put the class at ease, and don't avoid eye contact. Show your students that you're paying attention to them.

131

Roles people play

There are many different roles within a group. Some people act as caretakers and gatekeepers, maintaining a constructive working atmosphere. Others, unfortunately, don't. Here are just a few you might recognise!

- The Recognition Seeker tries to show own importance by boasting and excessive talking.

- The Topic Jumper continually changes the subject.

- The Withdrawer will not participate, but carries on private conversations within the group.

- The Blocker stubbornly disagrees and rejects others' views. Cites unrelated anecdotal experience.

- The Aggressor is highly critical of fellow students' work, but rarely reads out their own.

4.5 Assertiveness: protecting your own personal boundaries

Learning to be assertive does not mean becoming bossy, aggressive and self-centred. It does, however, help you to become more 'centred on yourself' in terms of becoming self-aware and self-directed. Assertiveness training challenges the old stereotypes of the passive/weak woman and the aggressive/macho man, and releases people to simply be themselves whilst at the same time taking responsibility for their relationships with others.

Non-assertiveness means:

- feeling physically tense and uncomfortable
- lacking self-respect
- being indirect and dishonest with self and others
- refusing to take responsibility for self and others
- lacking self-confidence and feeling insecure
- being afraid to say what you need and want from others.

Assertiveness means:

- feeling physically relaxed and comfortable
- showing respect for self and others
- being honest and direct with self and others
- taking responsibility for your own choices and decisions
- feeling self-confident and secure
- being able to be clear about your needs, wants and emotions.

The creative writing tutor must learn to be assertive for a number of reasons. Firstly, any teacher is in a position of power and must take responsibility for that. No matter how democratically you run your group, the bottom line is that (hopefully!) you are being paid, and often the students are contributing to your fee. This exchange is based on the assumption that you have something they want to buy, i.e. knowledge, guidance and expertise. Many writers who have not taught before find this balance of roles difficult to accept and try to undermine their own professional authority in order to be liked. Assertiveness training can be of assistance here because it helps you to define roles and boundaries, and shows you how to work within them.

Secondly, a writer working as a teacher has something else to protect — their own self-confidence and esteem. Writers tend to be rather isolated people who enjoy their own company and who are often at their most creative when they're inhabiting some distant nether-region of consciousness which excludes everyone else. To expect such a person to quit their piles of paper and stop staring at the wall in order to stand up in front of ten strangers is tantamount to requiring them to make friends with Vlad the Impaler, and certainly many writers would rather starve than teach. Those who do, therefore, should not be afraid to define their personal boundaries.

The most common threats to the writing tutor come from two main personality types: the sycophantic, and the envious. The sycophant will make you feel wonderful about yourself for a while, until you realise that having been awarded this extra esteem and power you are now expected to live up to your star status by reading extra manuscripts and attending family weddings and dinner parties. You can't say no, because then you will become a snobby star who's grown too big for their boots, so you reluctantly accept this unwanted adjunct to your social life (which, incidentally, reduces your writing time even more) and call it the price of fame. The envious student, on the other hand, is dedicated to digging out your bad reviews and secretly passing them round the class. They are jealous of your status and will try to demean it at every turn, pointing out syntax mistakes in your published works and leaping to correct you should you ever dare to make a mistake in front of the group. Worse, if you're not careful, the sycophant could turn jealous overnight and then you've got double trouble!

4.6   Should writers read?

Writers need readers, and readers need writers. However despite this most obvious fact it's true that, when quizzed, many beginner writers can barely remember the last book they read.

This is perhaps not so extraordinary as it might at first seem. After all, a vast number of people in the world know how to read — they can read billboards, and roadsigns, and instructions on food packets and electrical gadgets, and the TV page in the newspaper, and teletext on the screen. And, of course, they can also write.

'Everybody' can 'write'. They can write their names on cheques, and notes to the milkman, and holiday postcards. Many of us may have trouble making an accurate picture of a tree, but most people can spell the word 'tree', and we all know what it means, so where's the problem?

The problem, it could be said, lies in being able to describe, discuss and interpret that same tree, and it's here that the novice writer joins a long row of people queueing up to the Garden of Eden and beyond who have all at some time tried to do the same thing. In the *Oxford Dictionary of Quotations* there are 75 references to trees. Here are just a few:

Talking once more 'neath a swan-bosomed tree.

EDITH SITWELL, *1887-1964*

Fair pledges of a fruitful tree   ROBERT HERRICK, *1591-1674*

Trams and dusty trees.   T.S.ELIOT, *1888-1965*

He lieth under the shady trees   *Book of Job, The Bible*

(Why not ask your students to collect some more?)

To add to the confusion, there are different types of reading. (This would make a good topic for a class discussion.) The theorist Roland Barthes makes the distinction between 'readerly' texts, in which the reader gets caught up in the pleasure of the text and forgets that they are reading, and 'writerly' texts which force the reader to work at understanding and interpreting them, and are self-consciously 'written' without ever allowing the reader to sink into a simple enjoyment of the text.

So what do we use reading for? Perhaps as a pleasure drug, for relaxation or excitement; or as a soporific drug, to escape Reality; or to discover information, or as intellectual stimulation.

Many people were put off reading at school by élitist teachers who made them feel alienated and stupid because they did not appreciate 'The Classics'. Now is the time to assure your students that the fault lay at the door of the teacher for failing to enthuse them, and not with the pupils in need of help and guidance to understand the jokes in Chaucer or the beauty of a Shakespearian sonnet (see Section 2.5: Literary matters).

But, of course, it's never too late to start! The keyword here is PLEASURE. Encourage your students to:

- turn off the TV and curl up with a good book.
- laugh at the ending.
- put aside their lunch during the gory bits.
- make a guess at whodunnit.
- sob themselves to sleep with a romance.

I shall be like that tree, I shall die at the top.

JONATHAN SWIFT, 1667-1745

4.7 Maintaining and nurturing your own writing

Almost at the end of this book we come to the question you've probably been asking yourself all the way through — 'But do I really want to teach writing in the first place?'

The chances are that you're not sure.

The chances are that if someone offered you financial support for life you'd gleefully accept, kiss the classroom good-bye, and get on with writing your novel.

So let's be honest about this and come clean — most writers teach because they need the money. Oh yes, sometimes it can be enjoyable and very rewarding, but the bottom line is that it's supposed to free us to do our own writing.

Some writers vow that they will never succumb to the lure of teaching. They prefer to drive a fork-lift truck, or work in a sweet-shop, or eke out a living on tiny advances, rather than use up their creativity in the service of others. But some of us rather enjoy the lifestyle of a freebooting freelance author, Go Anywhere, Teach Anything, as long as it pays enough to fund six months' writing time. Except, of course, that six months soon dwindles to three and then to a day a week which you spend preparing lessons and reading other people's manuscripts.

Which brings us back again to the question of boundaries and self-protection. It's important to remember that the part of you which is the Writing Tutor is a different person to you the Writer. Keep the Writer at home, and don't expose it to the harsh light of the classroom. Don't allow it to be forced to explain or defend itself in public, don't allow it to answer complicated personal questions about motive, inspiration, or disappointment. Keep it well away from prying eyes.

- Don't allow teaching to sap your creative energies. Many promising poets, novelists and playwrights have taken the teaching route and disappeared into a black hole, never to be heard of again unless mentioned in book dedications by grateful protégés.

- Find a small area of your brain, programme it to teaching mode, and fence it off securely. When professionally required to use it you will find it fresh and ready to go, but make sure it's packed away again afterwards.

- Do not, repeat DO NOT, spend hours of your own writing time reading students' manuscripts. On occasion this is unavoidable, but make it the exception rather than the rule — unless, of course, you're being paid for the time you spend reading.

- Devote regular time and space to the things which feed you as a writer — good music, favourite authors, a special landscape, congenial people, solitude. These are not treats, they are an essential part of your creative life.

- Try not to let teaching become your sole source of income, and don't be seduced by flattery and success into taking every job you're offered.

- and NEVER STOP WRITING...

Writers
on
Teaching

KATHY PAGE

To write well, I believe it's necessary to either passionately enjoy or be compulsively attracted to writing for its own sake. You have to want to do it. A strong desire means that you'll be able to bear the set-backs that it entails and accept them as part of the process. A weak one means that you'll get fed up.

As a tutor/workshop leader I work from the assumption that everyone in the workshop is capable of writing well. This is not the same as saying that they will. Some workshop participants are experienced and talented writers already, others may show few signs of any kind of ability. The committed writer, prepared to listen but also to defend his or her work and intentions, is easy to encourage and often the learning is completely mutual.

In my experience the apparent non-writers in a group fall into two categories. The first contains people who have suffered disadvantage, or discouragement, or bad advice and so lack confidence and continually squash both themselves and their own work before someone else does: these are writers in waiting and they are extremely rewarding to teach. I'm always excited by the transformation of edgy silence into excitement: that moment when an individual who hasn't believed that they could have an 'idea' or 'anything to say' produces a first page or first paragraph and knows it is good. In a similar way, I feel very satisfied when someone who's been struggling makes perhaps drastic changes and cuts, transforming a confused story with a glimmer of interest into a working piece of fiction.

The other category of non-writer consists of the genuine non-writers: people who like the idea of being a writer far more than they enjoy the activity of writing itself, especially once they realise that writing involves rewriting, cutting, getting stuck, starting again: effort. The genuine non-writer often reads and writes very little but at the same time harbours grand fantasies of publication — even fame — and comes to the class so that the tutor will recognise his or her innate potential. Such students can be dazzled into some form of enthusiasm during the class or workshop, or encouraged to try new methods — but nothing ever sticks. They tend to become dependent on the tutor for starting points and feedback and indignant if they are not flattered. Handling the genuine non-writer is for me the most difficult part of teaching writing. I try to be honest and encourage them to see what, if anything, they can get from the activity of writing *per se*.

Students often ask whether I don't get sick of reading or listening to so many half-finished stories, novels without middles, plays with no dramatic tension and so on. Sometimes, on a residential course, ploughing through a pile of manuscripts at 2 a.m. can be a drag, but for the most part reading students' work is one of the best parts of the job, especially if it is good or shows progress on a previous draft, even if it's very rough. When students show a tutor work it is necessarily unfinished, in a state of flux: up for grabs. I enjoy putting my mind to it, seeing what's there and what the potential is: there's always some. No one ever learns 'to write', but only how to solve a particular writing problem in a particular context and thinking about other people's work is good mental exercise. There's a danger here though: that of trying to make the student do to the work what I would like to see done. This is pointless on two counts. In the first case he or she might not be able to do it and could end up discouraged. Secondly she or he is probably able to think of something far better or closer to their intentions. Carson McCullers wrote that a tutor should merely point out what works and what does not. I think she was probably right but I can't always stick to it.

It's very hard to teach writing well. You can teach particular craft skills (how to construct a scene or how to write dialogue) and you can encourage a writer's attitude to writing. The latter, which includes things such as learning to look after the part of you that produces ideas, developing the ability to criticise your own work, avoiding self-censorship, understanding the process of writing and so on is by far the most important.

If a writer is truly engaged with what she or he is writing, struggling to get it across, prepared to be honest about what parts are working and which are not, then that process will be remembered and will indirectly help with subsequent pieces. But because each writing problem is unique, formulae can't be applied: what you did in one situation probably won't work in the next. In addition, each student starts from a different point and each learns in the order that his or her interests dictate. I mean really learns: it's possible to understand something in theory, but that doesn't really count until it is practically applied. So I feel I have to teach many things on many levels at once, even in a group that has roughly the same competence.

Students can be eased into a more similar position on the learning curve if they're all encouraged to write, say, a particular kind of story in order to highlight a particular technical issue. But this can also be counterproductive: good writing begins from a powerful urge to explore and communicate. What is being said creates its own shape and to reverse the process can reduce engagement and thus the chances of success. The way to avoid this is of course not to be too doctrinaire about the exercises one offers. If a student has something else they are burning to do, I tell them, leave the exercise aside and do that instead.

I try to be flexible. It helps me to plan for a particular outcome, but because sessions always depend on input from the students that will rarely be the only outcome, and sometimes, as in writing itself, I end up completely elsewhere.

143

And sometimes I think that the most important thing I offer my students is simply enthusiasm, the fact that words — their words, mine, any — matter to me.

Kathy Page writes fiction and drama. Her latest novel is *Frankie Styne and the Silver Man,* published by Methuen, and her short stories are collected in *As in Music,* also Methuen. She has held numerous writer's residencies and currently teaches creative writing for the Open College of the Arts and at Birkbeck College.

5. Resources and Information

5.1 Marketing and publicity

Research

Decide how far you're prepared to travel in search of a class, and then spend some time investigating the existing provision. Make inquiries at libraries, adult education centres, colleges, community centres, and community arts projects — anywhere which may already be running a group.

You're looking for gaps in existing provision which you might be able to fill, and you're also searching for opportunities where you can create interest. Perhaps your local library has never thought of hosting a writing group before. Maybe the day centre for the elderly is desperate for activity ideas. Perhaps there is a clear need for a women-only group. Ask people about their preferred days and times. Term-time only? Winter or spring? Network by making contacts and talking to people, and keep clear notes of your findings.

You should also investigate sources of funding. Various agencies including Leisure Services Departments and Regional Arts Boards can advise you about grants and awards, and sometimes there is money available for special projects like rural development or ethnic arts.

Targeting

Your research will have shown you a) where the openings are, b) what people might be interested in, and c) where you might be able to obtain funding and what you would have to do to get it. You must make some decisions about the level at which you want to teach. Some classes are clearly more leisure-based than others. Are you comfortable with that, or would you prefer to teach a group with a fairly academic flavour? Of course there's no reason why you shouldn't run one of each. At this point you might like to remember that the country is already fairly well-peppered with classes in general creative writing. Can you offer something different, or more specialised? Use your research findings to clarify your ideas, and when you're ready, approach your target areas and offer something concrete for them to consider.

Libraries

Libraries very often have a spare room which they lend or hire to special interest groups. If you think you've found a suitable venue, approach the librarian in charge and sound them out about your project. They will probably want to know something about your suitability as a group leader and they may take some time to process their decision. Libraries make excellent venues in some respects because obviously you have access to books and a generally quiet working atmosphere. Disadvantages, however, include a ban on smoking and loud conversation, and in some cases restricted evening access.

Pubs, clubs and community centres

Pubs and clubs often have small meeting rooms available for hire, and tend to attract younger writers. The drawbacks are generally opposite to those of libraries — too much noise, too much smoke and alcohol — but at least you're not thrown out at 9.30 p.m.

Adult education

Most adult education centres and colleges of further education run classes in creative writing, and you can find information on these from their current prospectuses. Course planning tends to be done in early Spring, and by April or May most prospectuses are ready for the printers. It's useless, therefore, to approach a college in August when their advertising is underway and enrolments may have already begun. Bear in mind too that there is almost certainly going to be another writing tutor already in post, so you may be well-advised to offer a course which is either very different to or which complements existing provision. Incidentally, some colleges prefer tutors to have a recognised teaching qualification, whilst others don't insist upon it.

Others

Other openings will have been suggested to you by your research — prisons, hospitals, day-centres, workplaces, etc.

You've identified the market, now it's time to target your publicity.

Publicity

If you're lucky, you will receive an offer of work from a college or other institution and they will therefore be responsible for publicising and marketing your class. (Bear in mind, though, that a little additional publicity is never wasted.)

If, however, you have not been directly invited to run a group, you may need to start by convincing a funder or venue-manager to take you on. It's always useful to have a well-presented writer's CV detailing your publication record plus information about previous workshops, reading, etc. and including reviews, paper-cuttings and recommendations if you have them.

Publicising the class itself requires careful thought, and a certain amount of financial input. You will require two different types of publicity: one targeted at possible students and the other designed as a press release and aimed at local media who will hopefully then provide free advertising. Consider the following questions:

- what image will the group have: radical, intellectual, leisure, political, ethnic, gender-based, etc?
- who will be interested in enroling?
- where will they be likely to see my publicity?
- should I produce posters or handbills or both? How many?

- where should I send my press releases?
- how early will the media require them?
- should I organise a launch party or other publicity venture?

Schools

Many schools engage writers for half-day and whole-day workshops. This requires an entirely different needs analysis and marketing technique. Schools select and contact writers in one of two ways, either through the Education Library Service, which acts as a network point for all school librarians, or through members of staff themselves. Writers interested in working in schools should consider the following:

- do I want to do author readings, or run practical workshops, or both?
- does my work contribute to the National Curriculum? How?
- which age-groups do I want/not want to work with?
- do I prefer to work with Special Needs, A Level classes, etc?
- how many children and for how long? (Some teachers will offer you a hundred kids for a whole morning. Be polite, but say no.)

AND FINALLY... remember that publicity breeds more publicity, and more publicity breeds more work. Never turn down that photo-opportunity!

5.2 Money matters

It's extremely difficult to discover any minimum rates for tutors outside the formal education system. The figures below, therefore, have been gleaned from anecdotal evidence and should not be considered definitive in any way. They are presented simply as a guide for negotation and budgeting.

Further and higher education

Pay rates in further and higher education vary in respect of the subject offered and the degree of experience of the tutor. The current part-time rate runs between about £9 to £21 per hour. (A proportion of the part-time hourly rate covers preparation and marking.)

Schools, general groups and classes

Negotiable, but it's reasonable to expect an absolute minimum of £50 per half-day and £100 per full day. Longer-term residencies may be paid at a lower rate. It should also be possible to claim travel expenses.

Residential courses

Very variable. A typical weekend course runs from Friday evening to Sunday afternoon, whilst 'week-long' courses like Arvon run from Monday tea-time to Saturday morning. But remember that you will be working all the time, except when you are sleeping (and probably then as well!). 'Working' includes breakfast conversations about a student's writing, socialising in the evening, and reading manuscripts when everyone else has gone to bed. Payment is roughly £275 for a weekend and £400 for a week. Travel expenses are usually claimable, and of course your food and accommodation are free.

It's worth noting that institutions which run residential courses are often prepared to photocopy handouts, etc. for you, and frequently offer library facilities too.

Invoices

Unless you are on the payroll of a college or institution you will need to provide an invoice in order to be paid. If you have a word processor the easiest thing to do is to design a template invoice and then use it when needed.

Remember that your invoice sheet also acts as an advertisement for you, so make it as attractive and businesslike as possible. Scribbled entries in a blue carbon book from the newsagent don't set quite the right tone!

Inland Revenue: Schedule D

Schedule D covers people who are either fully or partly self-employed, and who do not pay PAYE but are taxed at the end of the financial year. Schedule D has certain advantages in terms of tax relief for travel expenses, materials, etc., but can also prove extremely inconvenient at times. Most educational establishments have no facility for paying visiting writers under Schedule D and tend instead to deduct tax at the highest rate. These deductions are reclaimable but involve complex paperwork and are responsible for some writers simply refusing to accept offers of work at such institutions.

National Insurance

It may be worth making enquiries about your individual situation regarding National Insurance Contributions. There are special arrangements for the self-employed who earn over a certain figure per year. Check with your local DSS office.

5.3 Copyright Law

An aspect of writing which worries new authors is the law regarding protection of copyright and intellectual property. Anxieties most commonly centre on the fear that unscrupulous editors, TV or radio producers are in a perfect position to plunder ideas from the hundreds of unsolicited creative pieces they receive every week. New writers generally do not have the protection of an agent, and they often feel highly vulnerable to this type of exploitation. And it's certainly true that although very few cases ever get to court it would be naïve to suggest that such theft never happens.

What is not covered by copyright law?

The law protects the form of the work, but not the underlying idea. This means that plots, the theft of which worries new writers the most, are not protected by the law. Nor are artistic ideas, themes and systems. In addition, works which are deemed too short to be literary works, e.g. advertising slogans, book and magazine titles, etc., are not accorded copyright protection.

Authors invited to meet producers and editors to 'chat through a few ideas' should therefore be aware that they may be giving away their ideas and expertise for no payment or acknowledgement whatsoever. A script or outline is of course protected by law, but the idea which informs it is not. Legal action would only be advisable, therefore, if the material development of the idea bears a very close resemblance to the original work.

Selling copyright

When selling a manuscript, authors should ask for details about the rights being purchased. Publishers often prefer to buy World Rights, whereas agents like to split them up and sell once in the UK then again in the USA, then offer the book for translation rights, film rights, and so on.

Permissions and fair dealing

There is another angle to copyright law, and that is the extent to which writers are allowed to use other writers' material in the form of quotations and extracts. A student who is interested in pop music, for example, may be unaware that the use of a single line of a famous lyric in a published short story could cost them a great deal in permissions fees.

Both published and unpublished works are protected by copyright for fifty years after the author's death. However, writers may quote another writer for 'purposes of criticism or review' if they give 'sufficient acknowledgement'.

It is wise to seek clarification about the use of an extract or quotation by applying for permission to use it. It may fall under 'fair dealing' — generally up to a total of 800 words, or up to a quarter of a poem — or payment might be required. The suggested minimum rate for prose is between £82 and £96 per 1,000 words for world rights for one edition only.

For the publication of poetry in anthologies the minimum fee is on a sliding scale beginning at £30 for the first 10 lines. Permissions for musical lyrics, incidentally, should be treated separately and tend to be more expensive.

Tutors and students wishing for specific information should obtain a copy of the Copyright, Designs and Patents Act 1988. Take note, too, that there are some very specific differences between UK and USA copyright laws.

5.4   Contact addresses

Arts Council of Great Britain 14 Great Peter Street, London SW1P 3NQ Tel: 071-333-0100. Funding and promotion of the arts.

Arvon Foundation Totleigh Barton, Sheepwash, Beaworthy, Devon EX21 5NS Tel: 0409-23338 and Lumb Bank, Heptonstall, Hebden Bridge, West Yorkshire HX7 6DF Tel: 0422-843714. Five-day residential courses for people of any age (16+) or background covering a wide range of literary forms.

Association of Little Presses 89a Petherton Road, London N5 2QT Tel: 071-226-2657. A loosely-knit association of individuals running little presses who have grouped together for mutual self-help, while retaining their right to operate autonomously.

Book Trust Book House 45 East Hill, Wandsworth, London SW18 2QZ Tel: 081-870-9055. Principal aim is to foster the growth of a wider and more discriminating interest in books.

British Fantasy Society 15 Stanley Road, Morden, Surrey SM4 5DE Tel: 081-540-9443. For writers and readers of fantasy and horror.

British Guild of Travel Writers 90 Corringway, London W5 3HA Tel: 081-998-2223. Arranges meetings, discussions and visits for its members (who are all professional travel writers) to help them encourage the public's interest in travel.

British Science Fiction Association Jo Raine, 33 Thornville Road, Hartlepool, Cleveland TS26 8EW. For readers and writers of science fiction and fantasy.

Comedy Writers' Association of Great Britain 24 Daresbury Road, Chorlton-cum-Hardy, Manchester M21 1WA. Tel: 061-881-9266. To develop and promote comedy writing in a professional and friendly way.

Community Arts Projects contact the relevant Regional Arts Board. For skills development and workshop opportunities.

Crime Writers' Association PO Box 172, Tring, Herts HP23 5LP. For professional crime writers.

Gay Authors Workshop Kathryn Byrd, BM Box 5700, London WC1N 3XX. To encourage writers who are lesbian or gay.

Institute of Journalists Unit 2, Dock Offices, Surrey Quays Road, London SE16 2XL Tel: 071-252-1187. Independent trade union of professional journalists.

National Association of Writers in Education (NAWE) 49 Byram Arcade, Huddersfield HD1 1ND Tel: 0484-452070. Professional association for writers working within an educational context.

National Poetry Foundation 27 Mill Road, Fareham, Hants PO16 0TH Tel: 0329-822218. The aim of the foundation is to provide a truly national poetry organisation which in turn provides a worthwhile appraisal system, plus advice, information, magazines and discussion documents.

156

National Union of Journalists Acorn House, 314 Gray's Inn Road, London WC1X 8DP Tel: 071-278-7916. Trade union for journalists.

P.E.N. International 38 King Street, London WC2E 8JT Tel: 071-379-7939. To promote friendship and understanding between writers and defend freedom of expression within and between all nations.

Poetry Society 21 Earls Court Square, London SW5 9DE Tel: 071-373-7861. A national body entirely devoted to the encouragement of poetry.

Regional Arts Boards

East Midlands Arts Mountfields House, Forest Road, Loughborough, Leicestershire LE11 3HU Tel: 0509-218292.

Eastern Arts Cherry Hinton Hall, Cherry Hinton Road, Cambridge, CB1 4DW Tel: 0223-215355.

London Arts Board Elme House, 133 Long Acre, Covent Garden, London WC2E 9AF Tel: 071-240-1313 + Helpline 071-240-4578.

Northern Arts 9-10 Osborne Terrace, Jesmond, Newcastle-upon-Tyne NE2 1NZ Tel: 091-281-6334.

North West Arts 12 Harter Street, Manchester M1 6HY Tel: 061-228-3062.

South East Arts 10 Mount Ephraim, Tunbridge Wells, Kent TN4 8AS Tel: 0892-515210.

South West Arts Bradninch Place, Gandy Street, Exeter EX4 3LS Tel: 0392-218188 Bristol Office: I Constitution Hill, Clifton, Bristol BS8 1DG Tel: 0272-253226.

Southern Arts 13 St Clement Street, Winchester SO23 9DQ Tel: 0962-855099.

West Midlands Arts 82 Granville Street, Birmingham B1 2LH Tel: 021-631-3121.

Yorkshire & Humberside Arts 21 Bond Street, Dewsbury, West Yorkshire WF13 1AX Tel: 0924-455555.

Romantic Novelists' Association 13 Manor Lane, Lewisham, London SE13 5QW Tel: 081-852-5067. To raise the prestige of romantic authorship.

Royal Literary Fund 144 Temple Chambers, Temple Avenue, London EC4Y 0DT Tel: 071-353-7150. To help professional writers and their families who face hardship. (The fund does not offer financial support for writing projects.)

Scottish Arts Council 12 Manor Place, Edinburgh EH3 7DD Tel: 031-226-6051. Funding and promotion of the arts in Scotland.

Screenwriters Workshop London 64 Church Crescent, London N10 3NE Tel: 081-883-7218. A forum for contact, discussion and practical criticism. Membership open to anyone ointerested in writing for film and television.

SCRIBO K.Sylvester, Flat 1, 31 Hamilton Road, Boscombe, Bournemouth BH1 4EQ Tel: 0202-302533. A friendly and informal postal forum for novelists.

Shape 27a Belvoir Street, Leicester, LE1 6SL Tel 0533-552933. For the promotion of disability arts.

Society of Authors 84 Drayton Gardens, London SW10 9SB Tel: 071-373-6642. Trade union and contact point for professional writers.

Society of Women Writers and Journalists 1 Oakwood Park Road, Southgate, London N14 6QB Tel: 081-886-2436. For women writers and artists. Lectures, monthly lunchtime meetings, free literary advice for members.

Verbal Arts Association Moira Monteith, School of Education, Sheffield Hallam University, 36 Collegiate Crescent, S10 2BP. Tel: 0742-720911. Professional association for writers working in higher education.

Welsh Arts Council Museum Place, Cardiff CF1 3NX Tel: 0222-394711. Funding and promotion of the arts in Wales.

Women Writers Network 55 Burlington Lane, London W4 3ET Tel: 081-994-0598. A forum for the exchange of information, support and career and networking opportunities for working women writers.

Writers' Circles *The Directory of Writers' Circles*, containing addresses and telephone numbers of several hundred writers' circles, guilds, workshops and literary clubs through the UK, is published regularly by Laurence Pollinger Ltd. It is available from compiler/editor Jill Dick (£3.00 post free) at Oldacre, Horderns Park Road, Chapel-en-le-Frith, Derbyshire SK12 6SY.

Writers' Guild of Great Britain 430 Edgware Road, London W2 1EH Tel: 071-723-8074. Trade union and contact point for professional writers.

5.4 Further reading

1. Teaching Adults

Teaching in Further Education LB Curzon, Holt Education, 3rd Edition 1985.

Adult Learning, Adult Teaching John Daines, Carolyn Daines & Brian Graham, Department of Adult Education, University of Nottingham 1992.

Teaching Skills in Further and Adult Education David Minton, Macmillan and City & Guilds, 1991.

Teaching Adults Alan Rogers, Open University Press, 1989.

2. Teaching Writing

Becoming a Writer Dorothea Brande, Papermac, 1934.

Fires Raymond Carver, Picador, 1985.

The Writing Life Annie Dillard, Picador, 1989.

Good English Guide Harry Fieldhouse, Dent, 1982.

Writing Down the Bones Natalie Goldberg, Shambhala, 1986.

The Complete Plain Words Sir Ernest Gowers, Penguin, 1962.

On Writing George V.Higgins, Bloomsbury, 1991.

Research for Writers Ann Hoffman, A & C Black, 1986.

Writing for the BBC Norman Longmate, BBC Books, 1988.